the culture engine

the culture engine

A FRAMEWORK FOR DRIVING RESULTS, INSPIRING YOUR EMPLOYEES, AND TRANSFORMING YOUR WORKPLACE

S. CHRIS EDMONDS

WILEY

For general information about our other products and services, please contact our Customer Care Department within the United States at (800) 762-2974, outside the United States at (317) 572-3993 or fax (317) 572-4002.

Wiley publishes in a variety of print and electronic formats and by print-on-demand. Some material included with standard print versions of this book may not be included in e-books or in print-on-demand. If this book refers to media such as a CD or DVD that is not included in the version you purchased, you may download this material at http://booksupport.wiley.com. For more information about Wiley products, visit www.wiley.com.

Library of Congress Cataloging-in-Publication Data:
Edmonds, S. Chris, 1952-
  The culture engine : a framework for driving results, inspiring your employees, and transforming your workplace / S. Chris Edmonds.
     pages cm
  Includes index.
  ISBN 978-1-118-94732-6 (hardback : alk. paper) ISBN 978-1-118-94733-3 (ebk);
ISBN 978-1-118-94734-0 (ebk)
  1. Employee motivation. 2. Strategic planning. 3. Leadership. I. Title.
  HF5549.5.M63E334 2014
  658.3′14–dc23
                                                                    2014023100

Printed in the United States of America

10 9 8 7 6 5 4 3 2 1

To my wife, Diane, and my family (especially Mom, Karin, and Greg, and Andy and Dana), who keep me on track with coaching, humor, and love.

This book is also dedicated to:

> My best (and worst) bosses, who taught me more about the impact of values in the workplace than any professor or any class could have.

> My culture clients, who accept my coaching (and prodding and pushing) with grace and enthusiasm as I help them create safe, inspiring work environments.

Special gratitude goes to Jerry Nutter (1938–2012), my greatest boss ever, who taught me volumes about values, culture, leadership, and workplace dignity.

CONTENTS

FOREWORD

I have been a big fan of Chris Edmonds for over 20 years—ever since I coaxed him into leaving the Federal Reserve Bank and joining our consulting partner group. Chris has been and continues to be one of our most requested consultants. One of the main reasons for this has been his deep interest in helping organizations produce high-performing cultures. I know few people who are better qualified to talk about this subject. Why? After you have read *The Culture Engine*, the answer will become clear: Chris understands what constitutes a culture that drives results and what it takes to make that culture come alive.

As a student and proponent of servant leadership, I love this book. When I mention servant leadership to many organizational leaders, they think I'm talking about the inmates running the prison, pleasing everybody, or some religious movement. What they don't understand is that there are two aspects of effective leadership. The first is the *strategic leadership* aspect of servant leadership. Leadership is about going somewhere. If your people don't know where you want them to go, there is little chance they will get there. That's why Chris spends a great deal of time helping you develop an organizational constitution that outlines your team's or company's purpose, values, strategies, and goals.

While there should be widespread involvement in the development of your organizational constitution, the responsibility for making sure you have one lies with top management. Once everybody is clear on your business purpose and values, the next aspect of effective leadership kicks in—living according to your organizational constitution. That involves turning the traditional hierarchical pyramid upside down to emphasize that everyone is responsible—*able to respond*— for living the constitution and getting the desired results while modeling the organization's valued behaviors. Now top management becomes responsive cheerleaders for actualizing the organizational constitution. This brings in the second, *servant* aspect of servant leadership—the operational/ implementation aspect.

While our research indicates that 80 to 85 percent of the impact on organizational vitality or success comes from operational leadership, without a clear organizational constitution there would be nothing to implement or serve. Chris believes in these two aspects of effective leadership—and so will you when you finish this wonderful book.

Thank you, Chris, for helping everyone who believes that culture trumps everything to make that belief a reality.

—Ken Blanchard

Coauthor of *The One Minute Manager*® and Cofounder and Chief Spiritual Officer of The Ken Blanchard Companies®

ACKNOWLEDGMENTS

I'm indebted to a number of people who have paved the way for this book.

Ken Blanchard has been a proactive supporter of mine for more than 20 years. I'm grateful for his belief in me as a thought leader, consultant, and speaker. My first experience with publishing was to contribute a chapter in the revised and enhanced edition of Ken's best seller, *Leading at a Higher Level*. Ken has been a beacon of brilliant light for me to follow and learn from.

My clients—those of my own firm and my Blanchard clients—have given me access to their most precious resource: the hearts and minds of leaders and team members in their organizations. I appreciate their willingness to let me be a disruptive force and to consider these ideas as they refine their organizational cultures. Thanks, too, to my sales colleagues who open the door to client opportunities for culture refinement.

Matt Holt and Shannon Vargo at John Wiley & Sons have been champions of this book project since the moment they reviewed the proposal. I'm grateful for their enthusiasm, professionalism, and diligence to help me get these ideas into print and into the hands of leaders around the globe. Thanks also to Liz Gildea, editorial assistant, for her willing guidance and support of this project.

Mark Levy is a vital member of my branding brain trust. I appreciate Mark's humor, passion, clarity, and wide knowledge base of publishing, branding, and the New York Mets. Mark helped me find my sweet spot – championing an organizational constitution. Mark helped me refine my brand, my voice, and this book concept, and he continues to open doors for me today. Mark made this book a reality and I'm indebted to him.

Last but not least, I'm grateful for the love and support of my lovely bride (of 35 years), Diane. She has blessed this crazy dream of mine to publish these concepts and build a career helping organizations be better places to hang out.

INTRODUCTION

Is your workplace frustrating and lifeless, or is it engaging and inspiring?

When you think of your work environment, what descriptors come to mind?

For many people, descriptors such as "dreary," "discouraging," "fear-based," and "missed promises" apply to their organization's culture.

Today, people spend more time at work than with their best friends or family members. When the workplace is an inspiring, respectful, creative place to be, people engage deeply, serve customers effectively, and produce quality goods and services consistently.

The problem? Most leaders put greater thought into their organization's products and services than they do its culture. Yet culture is the engine—it drives everything that happens in an organization each day.

Leaders don't want a dreary or frustrating organizational culture, but most don't know what to do about it. They've seen inspiring workplaces but have never been taught how to create or maintain one.

Of course, understanding the need for a safe, inspiring culture is one thing. Creating and managing a productive, engaging culture is another thing entirely.

How does a leader go about creating something that, on one hand, is so important, but, on the other hand, seems so amorphous?

It can be done through the creation of an organizational constitution.

An organizational constitution is a formal document that states the company's guiding principles and behaviors. These liberating rules present the best thinking on how the organization wants to operate. The constitution is a North Star that outlines the company's or team's defined playing field for employee performance and values.

Stephen Covey said that a personal "mission statement becomes a *personal constitution* [italics mine], the solid expression of your vision and values."[1] Marcus Luttrell, former U.S. Navy SEAL and author of *Lone Survivor*, said in that book, "As with many big corporations which have a dedicated workforce, you can tell a lot about them by their corporate philosophy, their *written constitution* [italics mine], if you like. It's the piece of writing which defines their employees and their standards."[2]

Your organizational constitution builds on this foundational understanding of the power of formal, liberating rules for citizenship, values, and teamwork. An organization's constitution is the solid expression of its purpose and values, of its corporate philosophy.

Your organizational constitution describes exactly how its members will engage with each other, suppliers, vendors, and customers, as members act to fulfill their organization's purpose, values, strategies, and goals.

An organizational constitution outlines your team's purpose, values, strategies, and goals. It paints a vivid picture of success, values, and behaviors. It maps out how to work from that picture each day.

An organizational constitution gives employees' jobs and roles meaning and clarity.

The organizational constitution eliminates unspoken assumptions. There is no more confusion about what the "integrity" value really means or why a decision was made (or not).

Through their organizational constitution, leaders make expectations explicit and describe what a good job and a good citizen look like in specific, tangible, observable terms.

Once your organizational constitution is written and shared, leaders can live by it, lead by it, and manage to it. Your constitution provides the organization's managers and employees a clear understanding of how they can do their best work, treat others respectfully, and help the organization prosper.

This is what *The Culture Engine* is about: it teaches you how to formalize liberating rules that transform your work environment from frustrating and lifeless to engaging and inspiring.

How Did I Learn about Organizational Constitutions?

Forty-five years ago I joined the workforce. I've had a lot of jobs. I've had some good bosses—and some lousy bosses, too.

One of my lousy bosses made grand promises—to staff, to volunteers, and to customers. Yet he kept few of his commitments. I learned that his word was not trustworthy.

Another lousy boss was skilled at pointing out my mistakes and failures, but he was quiet when I exceeded expectations and moved the organization forward. I learned to insulate myself from his presence because all I heard from him was disappointment.

My worst boss asked me to lie. My staff and volunteers raised $25,000 in my first year as branch executive, double what that branch had ever raised before. At the campaign's closing dinner, with 300 people in attendance, my boss told me to announce that we had raised $30,000. I refused and announced our actual total. My boss wasn't happy. Neither was I. I left that job as quickly as I could.

It took one great boss to open my eyes to the power of organizational culture. Jerry created a team of high performers who exceeded performance standards while, at the same time, demonstrating great team citizenship. Jerry set high standards for values, outlining how team members were to behave to ensure we were modeling our team's values.

Jerry paid attention to more than our performance traction and accomplishments—he paid attention to how we treated each other and how we treated customers. He called us on our bad behavior promptly and cheered our aligned behaviors loudly.

During this time, Jerry handed me the project of a lifetime. He wanted me to take the ideas he used to build his staff team's culture and apply them to YMCAs in the country's roughest neighborhoods.

I went to YMCAs in South Central Los Angeles, San Diego, and San Francisco, cities that had heavy teen gang presences. Some of the kids in these gangs were drug users. Others were into prostitution, robbery, even murder.

It was our job to make the YMCA a compelling enough place so that teens would leave their lives of crime and violence.

We created a strategy built upon what teenagers want: a sense of belonging, cool activities, and meaningful contribution. These same wants explain why kids are attracted to gangs.

Slowly, our ideas on creating a more inviting culture started taking hold. YMCAs began seeing teenagers return to their programs and buildings.

Some of the kids became Y-camp counselors, bus drivers, and camp directors. Others became YMCA program directors; a few went on to become YMCA executives.

I remember one kid in particular. He told us he had been a member of a street gang. But he was intrigued by cool happenings at his local YMCA, so he joined the California Youth & Government program. In Youth & Government, he learned parliamentary procedure, wrote bills, and served as a legislator in the actual Capitol facilities.

His finest moment was standing on the floor of the California Assembly in a borrowed suit, passionately presenting his bill to his Assembly peers. He was articulate, inspiring, confident—and immensely proud when his bill passed the house.

Jerry taught me how powerful a great culture is for driving performance and values alignment (or not, in the case of a lousy culture).

Jerry also taught me that aligned behaviors are the pathway to workplace inspiration—and that misaligned behaviors lead to workplace frustration.

I was so transformed by my experiences with Jerry that I wanted to expand those ideas out as far as I could. I figured that if having a more values-aligned culture could turn around gang members, perhaps it could work in other places.

Over 25 years ago I started teaching these same principles to organizations, divisions, departments, and teams, helping them clarify their organizational constitutions, helping bosses be great, and helping to build engaging, inspiring workplaces.

This book presents best practices of high-performing, values-aligned work environments. It provides insights from my decades of experience and research on proven ways leaders can craft a safe, respectful, dignified workplace where employees thrive.

It pulls back the curtain and reveals how to refine your team's or company's culture—your company's engine and work environment—so your people feel trusted, valued, and engaged in wowing customers every day.

How Is the Book Structured?

The book is organized around three themes: defining an organizational constitution, crafting your organizational constitution, and managing to your organizational constitution.

The first theme, defining an organizational constitution, resides in Chapter 1. In this first chapter, you'll learn the elements of an organizational constitution and why you need one for your company, division, department, or team.

The second theme, crafting your organizational constitution, is found in Chapters 2 through 5. In these chapters, you'll learn how to create your personal constitution as well as how to create your organizational constitution, using real client examples and worksheets to craft each element.

The third theme, managing to your organizational constitution, resides in Chapters 6 through 10. In these chapters, you'll learn how to demonstrate, measure, and coach others to embrace your organizational constitution, bringing values to life in daily interactions.

Engage in this process! With it, you can change your work environment from dreary and frustrating to inspiring, fun, and productive.

You're going to be in your role, anyway, right? You may as well build workplace inspiration while you're there.

Let's learn how to refine your culture engine and implement this constitution thing.

CHAPTER 1

What Is an Organizational Constitution and Why Do You Need One?

You sense it the moment you step onto the Southwest Airlines plane.

Flight attendants greet you with a hearty, "Welcome aboard!" They look you squarely in the eye and give you a big smile.

One asks how your day has been and genuinely listens to your answer as they walk with you up the aisle to your chosen seat.

What you sense and feel so readily is that Southwest Airlines employees *care*. They enjoy what they do. They enjoy their teammates. They enjoy their customers.

They willingly engage with customers and teammates and have fun with both. And, they have fun while flying customers safely to their destinations, consistently on time (arrivals and departures), and with one of the lowest incidences of lost luggage in the industry.

Southwest delivers top performance while serving customers happily.

Or, you may be shopping on Zappos.com. You don't see the shoe model you'd like online so you call their toll-free phone number (which is prominently displayed on every page). As you dial, you realize it's 1:00 a.m.

No worries. Zappos team members are available 24/7. Carmen answers the phone and cheerily asks how she can help you. You explain that the website doesn't show the shoe you're looking for.

Carmen says, "Let's see if I can find a shoe that you might love!" Within moments, Carmen suggests two models with similar features and styling. She points you to their web page on Zappos.com so you can view them and decide if you'd like to try them.

You tell Carmen you would like to "hold them in your hands." She arranges free shipping of both pairs so you can try them on at home.

Carmen says, "Keep the pair you love, and ship the other pair back to us. Free!" She explains that if you don't like either pair, ship them both back for a full refund.

Zappos delivers top performance while serving customers happily.

Both of these successful, service-driven, and unique companies have *formalized their purpose and values.*

They are intentional about workplace inspiration. They don't leave their company culture—or the treatment of employees and customers—to chance.

Southwest Airlines staff and Zappos team members engage willingly, pleasantly, and enthusiastically with customers because *they love serving people.* Southwest Airlines and Zappos hire people with a service mindset and a servant heart. Team members who don't embrace the values of these organizations don't stay.

In these organizations, there is no space for team members who don't align with the company's values and who don't enjoy serving others.

You may have experienced other providers that have "it," that unique, friendly, authentic, inviting environment that envelops you as a customer.

It might be your favorite "mom and pop" espresso house or your local dry cleaners.

You might not stop to think about it; you might just bask in it!

And, maybe you have thought about it.

You've asked yourself, "How do they do that? How do they create such an inspiring workplace that includes employees who love their work and love their customers?"

What companies like Southwest Airlines and Zappos do is make workplace inspiration—the employee experience—as important as performance and profits.

WHAT IS THE CONDITION OF YOUR TEAM OR COMPANY'S CULTURE, RIGHT NOW?

Just as you can sense the customer-focused culture when stepping onto a Southwest Airlines plane or speaking with a Zappos customer service team member, you can gauge the culture of your team or company by walking around your operation, by listening to what is important to staff, and by observing the quality of interactions between leaders, followers, and customers.

I encourage you to pay attention to what you pay attention to.

Most leaders look exclusively at profits and production.

And, results are not the only important product of an organization. How people are treated—and how they treat others—is a vitally important element of workplace inspiration that needs proactive and intentional tending.

Leaders of teams and companies need to keep their fingers on the pulse of *how* their organization is operating, not just how it's performing.

In each chapter, you will find a Culture Effectiveness Assessment that will require you to learn your organization's "truth," in order to check your assumptions about what is and is not going well within your team or company.

Leaders base plans, decisions, and actions on what they believe to be true about their team or company "in the moment." To what extent, though, do leaders check their beliefs against others' perceptions before making a decision or taking an action?

This book is designed to help educate leaders and team members about what a high-performing, values-aligned work environment looks, acts, and feels like. The book includes tools like the Culture Effectiveness Assessment, step-by-step ways to craft each element of your organizational culture, and proven guidelines for how to communicate, market, and manage to your organizational constitution.

Each of these elements is designed to make you hyper-focused on both your team or company's performance and the values it lives by. The examples, stories, and tools presented in this book will help you to learn your organization's truth and the reality of how the workplace environment operates today.

To understand your organization's truth, you need to:

- **De-Insulate Yourself.** It is likely that you have, unintentionally, depended upon a select few players to give you information about what's happening around your workplace daily. Increase the number of your sources inside the company. Dedicate space and time to learn from different players throughout the organization to ensure you're getting a bigger, more accurate picture.

- **Genuinely Connect with Team Members.** Employees know which leaders are truly interested in them as people, not just in them as contributors or "cogs in a wheel." Connect with players in every department and function. Learn people's names. Engage them in conversations about their families and hobbies. Take five minutes to visit, without problem solving. Listen without defending. Over time, these genuine connections will enable others to tell you their perceptions, concerns, and hopes.

- **Seek Out Truth-Tellers.** It is all too common for leaders to, over time, surround themselves with people who reinforce the leader's current beliefs and perceptions. However, the most effective leaders engage with truth-tellers often. Truth-tellers are unafraid of describing their perceptions, theirs and others' understanding of the reality of the leader's plans, decisions, and actions. Knowing more people's truths can help make the leader's future decisions more effective.

- **Share Your Assumptions and Your Learning.** Check your assumptions by sharing them with team members. Say, "I believe x is an opportunity for us. What do you think?" As you learn more of your organization's truths, share those. Say, "I'm learning that many of you don't understand a recent decision of mine. Here's what I was trying to accomplish . . . ." Listen, and continue to refine your assumptions, plans, decisions, and actions.

In the meantime, we need you to learn more about what's happening in your work environment today. To help you start to understand your organization's "truth," I encourage you to take a tour, right now, of your team or company's work environment.

Don't take notes. Just wander around, and observe the current state of your team or company culture. (You can jot notes down later.)

On your tour, notice whether the work environment is clean, bright, and inviting.

Notice if workspaces and hallways are free of any material that might cause someone to stumble or that inhibits free and safe passage.

Is signage helpful and clear?

Does the facility and equipment "shine" with loving care, or is it dull from years of use and neglect?

Do employees greet each other kindly, not so kindly, or not at all (they mostly ignore each other)?

How do employees greet customers (if yours is a customer-interfacing environment)?

How do team members treat each other—with respect, with distain, or something in between?

Are team members doing the work they need to be doing—or are they distracted?

Is the work environment one of steady activity, frantic activity, or something in between?

How are customers referred to—as valued partners or "distractions" to getting the "real work" done?

Observe meetings, paying close attention to plans, decisions, and actions. Do those plans, decisions, and actions honor employees, customers, and stakeholders equally—or does one group win out over the others?

Take in every function during your tour. Observe behavior and conditions all over your facility. Take notes on your insights.

If you have facilities located in far-flung regions, you can phone people you trust in those facilities and ask them to tour, observe, and report back their insights.

Before we review your tour notes and insights, let me congratulate you. You've just done something that far too few leaders do examine the condition of your organization's culture. These culture tours are vital ways for you to keep tabs on how well your culture operates, how inspiring your work environment is, and the degree to which employees are excited to serve in and for your company or team.

The best way—our proven way—for you grow skills for proactive culture management is to:

- Study the best practices of high-performing, values-aligned organizations (which this book and other avenues provide).

- Gather frequent data on the condition of your team or company's culture (through observation, employee surveys, exit interviews, frequent informal conversations, and other means).

- Close identified gaps between your current culture and the high-performance, values-aligned culture you and your employees deserve.

If you choose to proactively manage your desired team or company culture—and I'm confident you will (after all, you're reading this book right now)—you'll be doing more tours more often in the days to come.

Let's review your tour insights by having you rate the statements in the chart that follows on a one to six scale. Circle your score for each item.

Culture Effectiveness Assessment #1: Informal Tour	Strongly Disagree	Disagree	Slightly Disagree	Slightly Agree	Agree	Strongly Agree
1. **Workspace Attractiveness** Our work environment is bright, clean, and inviting.	1	2	3	4	5	6
2. **Workspace Safety** Our work environment delivers safe passage and safe operations.	1	2	3	4	5	6
3. **Team Member Perceptions and Interactions** Leaders and team members enjoy positive, trusting relationships with each other daily.	1	2	3	4	5	6
4. **Team Member Performance** Team members know what they're supposed to do and are actively engaged in doing it daily.	1	2	3	4	5	6
5. **Customer Perceptions and Interactions** Internal and external customers are treated with the utmost dignity and respect during every interaction.	1	2	3	4	5	6

Tally up your scores. On this first assessment, the total possible point value is 30. A score of 25–30 is very good; that means you rated each item with "agree" or "strongly agree."

It is likely that your total score at this early stage is short of 25 points—maybe even short of 15.

You may be a "tough grader," holding your team or company to high standards. That's not a bad thing here.

You may be an "easy grader," believing your team is terrific, despite the reality that is evident just below the surface.

You need the perspective of the *unvarnished truth*, a clear understanding of your team or company's true starting point in this journey toward a high-performing, values-aligned workplace.

Whether you scored your team or company culture as effective or not so effective at this stage, you probably believe your team or company is performing below it's potential. You've seen opportunities pass the team by, maybe because they weren't ready for it . . . or they couldn't see the opportunity for themselves . . . or they didn't want to work any harder . . . or a multitude of other reasons. "Why wouldn't the team see this opportunity?" you might ask.

You probably see self-serving behavior by leaders or employees, periodically or more frequently. "Why do those players act in self-serving ways?" you might ask.

These are a wonderful, insightful example of the "concept of perfection."

THE CONCEPT OF PERFECTION

In the executive coaching world, the concept of perfection can help clients understand that there are very good reasons for why things are the way they are and why things happen the way they do.

In this case, perfection doesn't mean that things are working "perfectly" or "as desired." It means they are working *exactly the way we should expect them to work*, desirable or not.

In an executive coaching relationship, a coach tries to help a client understand that their behavior, decisions, and actions are logical, rational outcomes of their beliefs and thoughts. The situation they find themselves in at any point in time is entirely driven by their behavior, decisions, and actions up to that point.

This is a cause-and-effect circumstance. The cause (the client's beliefs and thoughts) leads directly to the effect (the client's behavior, decisions, and actions).

A coach can easily see how the resulting effect is entirely driven by the underlying cause. The results are "perfect." A person wouldn't expect to see any different behaviors, decisions, or actions, given that client's core beliefs and thoughts.

In a culture coaching relationship, a consultant (yours truly, for example) tries to help leaders understand that the team or company's culture—the way members behave, decide, and act—are logical, rational outcomes of the leader's beliefs and thoughts about the business and the people in their business.

The concept of perfection is a powerful tool to help leaders assess their organization's culture. A company's culture evolves over time based upon the beliefs and thoughts of its leaders (cause), and that logically leads to consistent behavior, decisions, and actions demonstrated by members that live in that company's culture (effect).

Let's say that in your team or company you experience caring leaders who demonstrate trust and respect for their team members and who celebrate successes and wins along the way. You are seeing those leaders' underlying beliefs and thoughts being played out in that culture. It is *perfect*.

Or, in your team or company, you experience leaders who take credit for your work, who pit employees against each other, and who rejoice in "catching people doing things wrong." You are seeing those leaders' underlying beliefs and thoughts being played out in that culture. It, too, is perfect.

If you experience "less than positive" behaviors, decisions, and actions in your organization's culture, understand that *people are acting exactly as you would expect*. The way they are behaving now is being reinforced consistently, albeit maybe unintentionally.

If you want to eliminate negative behaviors, decisions, and actions in your organization's culture, you must change what gets reinforced.

You must *define* a "better way." Then, you must *live* the better way, every interaction. You must measure how all leaders are perceived, asking employees to regularly rank leaders on the degree to which they model your team or company's desired purpose, values, behaviors, strategies, and goals.

If you want more positive behaviors, decisions, and actions in your organization's culture, you must begin work to change the underlying expectations of leaders in your organization.

This is exactly what an organizational constitution does.

HOW CIVIL IS YOUR WORKPLACE?

Now that you understand how the concept of perfection is at work, every minute of every day, reinforcing your current workplace environment, let's look at the five levels of workplace inspiration.

In my research and experience I have found that every team and company culture I observe fits into one of these levels. From lowest to highest, the levels of workplace inspiration are:

- Dysfunction

- Tension

- Civility

- Acknowledgment

- Validation

A *dysfunctional* culture would be evidenced by open conflict and disagreement, rude treatment of employees and customers, and managing by intimidation. Workplace teasing and bullying is common at this level.

In a *tension-filled* culture, cliques isolate select employees. Jokes of a sexual or political nature are shared verbally or by email. Roles and efforts are undermined. Gossip is prevalent. Blaming and finger pointing can be seen daily. Teasing and bullying also happens at this level.

Civility is the first of these levels where consistent sanity is the norm. Work relationships are professional, formal, and diplomatic, if distant. The work environment is psychologically safe and respectful.

At the *acknowledgment* level, authentic respect is communicated often. Leaders and team members proactively thank peers for their efforts and their accomplishments. Credit is given willingly.

The *validation* level is the highest degree of workplace inspiration. Not only is credit given for efforts and accomplishment, responsibility and authority is given to engaged, talented team members. Players act independently and cooperatively to move the organization forward and deliver top-quality products and services. People smile frequently, engage their peers respectfully, and feel trusted and valued.

Just as the concept of perfection reinforces a less-than-desirable work environment, it can also create and reinforce the desired validating work environment. It's all up to the leader, who must be intentional about their desired culture (defining it through an organizational constitution), then reinforcing that validating work environment every minute of every day.

There is an interesting dynamic that is very common in the dysfunctional or tension-filled levels: workplace bullying. As you can imagine, bullying has a powerful negative impact on workplace inspiration.

Research indicates that workplace bullying is part of many work environments around the world. Monster.com's 2011 global poll[1] found that *two-thirds of respondents admit to being victims of workplace bullying*. In addition, this study found that half of respondents who have not been bullied have witnessed it in the workplace.

The Canadian Centre for Occupational Health and Safety[2] reports that people who are the targets of workplace bullying may suffer from:

- Shock
- Anger
- Feelings of frustration and/or helplessness
- Physical symptoms, like the inability to sleep or a loss of appetite
- Psychosomatic symptoms such as stomach pains or headaches
- Family tension or stress
- Low morale and poor productivity

Bullying affects the workplace in broader ways, as well, through:

- Increased absenteeism and turnover
- Poor customer service

- Increased frequency of accidents and reportable incidents

- Increased costs of employee assistance programs (EAPs)

Your team or company cannot afford to reside in the dysfunctional or tension-filled levels. You must build a work environment of civility, acknowledgement, or validation—without delay.

We'll use the Culture Effectiveness Assessment—asking you to rate your team or company culture with questions in each chapter—to gauge your organization's level of workplace inspiration.

And, we'll outline steps to follow to help your team or company's work environment evolve.

WHO IS IN CHARGE OF CULTURE?

Helping your team or company's culture evolve into a validating, consistently high-performing and values-aligned work environment is a lot of work.

Culture change or, if you prefer, culture *refinement* is not something to be taken casually. It must be seen as vital work that needs time, energy, and intention to help craft consistent workplace inspiration.

So, who must lead your team or company's culture shift?

The player or players who are responsible for culture change are those who:

- Can create or modify the organization's incentives, policies, and procedures, and

- Have formal authority to guide the team, department, division, or company

In short, the leaders of your team or company are in charge of your team or company's culture.

Leaders get the credit when they have crafted a safe, inspiring, and productive work environment. Leaders also (deservedly) get the blame when they have crafted a tense, fear-driven, "I win, you lose" work environment.

However your team or company's culture is operating today, it's "perfect," exactly as we'd expect it to be.

If leaders want that culture to evolve, they must take action to *clarify* their desired culture (defining it in behavioral terms), *model* their desired culture (living it in every interaction), and *hold everyone on the team or in the company accountable* for living it in every interaction.

Here's the challenge: Most leaders have not *experienced* successful culture change. Even fewer have *led* a successful culture change.

Most team or company leaders simply don't know how to proactively manage their organization's culture.

That's what this book is designed to do—it educates leaders about a proven path for designing and aligning their desired culture.

The absence of demonstrated skills in managing a team or company's culture can tempt leaders to delegate the responsibility and authority for culture management to someone else in the organization.

Sometimes this temptation is driven by the absence of interest on a leader's part, so they delegate culture responsibility and authority.

Culture responsibility is often delegated to human resources or organization development or a similar function.

Delegation of culture responsibility almost always results in the complete failure of the culture change to gain traction. Why? Because only leaders of a team or company:

- Can create or modify the organization's incentives, policies, and procedures, and
- Have formal authority to guide the team, department, division, or company

If leaders are serious about culture change, they must accept, even embrace, the responsibility for it. To effectively guide their team or company's culture refinement, leaders must follow the guidance of proven practitioners (like yours truly) so their desired culture comes to fruition. This book provides that guidance.

NUTTERISMS

I introduced you to Jerry Nutter, one of my best bosses, in this book's introduction. He often taught us through truisms—which we called *Nutterisms*. I'll share some of these with you in features throughout the book.

"Everything a leader does either helps, hurts, or hinders the creation of a great team culture."

Leaders don't have neutral impact. They are on duty 24/7. Effective leaders are present, thoughtful, inquisitive, and of service, every moment.

CREATE A POCKET OF EXCELLENCE

What if you're not the CEO of your organization? Can you change the culture of *just* your team—even when it exists in a "less than perfect" broader organizational culture?

Many of you reading this book are not chief executive officers of your company.

Your "sphere of influence" may include a plant, a division, a department, or simply your own functional team.

Is it *possible* to institute an organizational constitution and make a positive difference in your sphere of influence, to build workplace inspiration?

Absolutely!

Is it *worth* it to engage your team or department in this process, when the overall parent organization isn't engaging in culture change at the same time?

Absolutely!

Many of the clients I've worked with over the past 20 years have been smaller, distinct units of their broader organization. They were plants, divisions, departments, and teams.

The leaders of those units realized the culture of their unit just wasn't helping their team's performance nor was it inspiring team members to bring their best and do their best, consistently.

A catalog printing plant came to our process because they scored so low on their company's employee engagement survey. They were told they *had* to "fix it," but weren't told *how* to fix it. They found us.

A large retailer came to us because the new senior vice president wasn't getting the quick traction he wanted on his vision, which was, "People with Passion drive Performance!"

One client implemented our process with his functional team. He had no budget but he did have time and an understanding of our best practices. The work with his team was "below the radar," not apparent to the rest of his division or the larger organization around him.

This leader simply brought his team along on the constitution journey.

Each of these units was a part of a larger organization or parent company. In most cases, the larger organization thought the culture work they were doing was, well, *dumb*. "How much money are you spending on this culture thing?" these unit leaders were asked. "Why are you wasting your time on culture? You won't see any benefit," they were told.

The questions kept coming until the impact of the culture shift became clear.

When tangible benefits such as 35 percent gains in profits and 40 percent gains in customer ratings and 40 percent gains in employee engagement are realized, the questions seem to go away.

Tangible benefits usually occur within 6 to 12 months of starting the culture refinement. When leaders stay on the path, fully implementing their organizational constitution, even greater benefits occur, typically in a timeframe of 18 months to 3 years.

Such pockets of excellence are a delight to behold. We've all seen them in our organizations over time. We observe their success, their unique teamwork, and think, "I wonder why that team is doing so well—and having so much fun? What is their leader doing to create that?"

Then we go about our business, not giving it another thought. We don't stop and pursue how these "pockets of excellence" operate.

You can create a pocket of excellence, starting now. You can craft a team (or department or division or company) culture that inspires high performance and exceptional, respectful teamwork. You can build a team that loves its work, its customers, and its team spirit.

Whether you are doing culture refinement with a large or small team, you must embrace the role of proactive culture champion. You must invest time and energy in the communication, coaching, and celebration of traction towards your desired culture.

This book will outline the phases and steps required to create an organizational constitution and align people, plans, decisions, and actions to it. Implementing these strategies will help your team or company culture to evolve into a high-performing, values-aligned workplace.

An Organizational Constitution Is a "Disruptive Technology" in Your Workplace

This book is a road map for the creation of an inspiring organizational culture that generates organizational success (performance and profits) while, at the same time, honors its people through a work environment of safety, trust, dignity, and respect.

The foundation of workplace inspiration, of high performance and values alignment, is an organizational constitution.

To a great extent, implementing an organizational constitution in your team or company is a *disruptive technology*—it introduces new ways and new demands into an organization that is comfortable with its old ways. It causes pain and confusion as people leave behind what "has been okay around here" and embracing what you, the leader, "want it to be like around here."

Creating the clear expectations and liberating rules of an organizational constitution will take time and energy. It will also take time and energy to communicate, model, and reinforce these expectations over time.

Shifting your team or company culture from "what is" to "high performance and values aligned" will disrupt routines, power structures, and stupid policies. It will create unintended consequences—some good, some not good at all.

It's a disruption, but the shift to a safe, inspiring, and respectful work environment is worth the short-term discomfort. Right?

So, what is an organizational constitution, exactly?

An organizational constitution is like the Magna Carta or United States Constitution in that it outlines specific expectations and rights of organizational members (leaders and employees).

Unlike the Magna Carta or U.S. Constitution, an organizational constitution does *not* outline the *governance* of the organization (employee ownership and such). It *does* describe the proven elements that make an organization's work environment consistently safe, respectful, productive, and inspiring.

An organizational constitution is a living, breathing document that outlines clear agreements on the team or company's purpose and the values and behaviors that all team leaders and members believe in and commit to.

The deeper that leaders drive their organizational constitution into their team, department, division, facility, or organization, the better the impact: higher employee engagement, wowed customers, and boosted profits.

When you manage by an organizational constitution, your team or company culture changes for the better, driven by *liberating rules* that leaders and employees buy into and demonstrate daily. These rules help them through ambiguity, setting standards of great team citizenship as well as great team performance.

When organizations don't have a constitution, people can behave badly—despite having the best of intentions. Players are simply trying to deliver what has been asked of them, using any means possible.

I hear about these scenarios in client organizations nearly every week.

Let me give you an example. Two senior leaders of a small professional services firm found themselves in a heated argument in the corporate offices, in full view of more than 40 staff members.

One demanded that a big client receive special treatment. The other argued that creating exceptions makes it hard to keep track of agreements and commitments. She explained how exceptions lead to missed promises more often than not.

In minutes they were berating each other using profanity that would make a longshoreman blush. They both stormed off, with no resolution on the issue. Anxious staff members looked at each other, embarrassed.

I spoke to the CEO who managed these two senior leaders. I asked, "Why do you tolerate such bad public behavior from your leaders?"

[Silent pause.]

The CEO said, "I told them to stop, but they keep doing it."

I explained, "Well, telling them doesn't seem to eliminate the lousy behavior, does it?"

[Another silent pause.]

I said, "Let's talk about changing the rules of engagement around here. Would it be helpful to outline standards of behavior that would be respectful of everyone?"

"Sure," the CEO said, "that'd be great."

"Drafting the agreements is easy. Aligning everyone's behavior is a little harder. But, that's your primary job as CEO," I coached.

This CEO's company needed rules of civility, acknowledgement, and validation embedded in a formal organizational constitution. And, this CEO's company needed to manage to those performance and values standards, consistently.

Margaret Wheatley, the best-selling author and management consultant, states that, "Aggression is the most common behavior used by many organizations."[3] She sees aggression as "a nearly invisible medium that influences all decisions and actions" in a team or company. The problem is that aggression is "one of the greatest barriers to thinking clearly and working well together."

Aggression inhibits high performance and the alignment of values.

An organizational constitution redefines what a "good job" looks like for leaders and employees in your company or team. Most organizations focus entirely on results and performance. Results are certainly important, as financial viability helps the organization succeed another day. But, results aren't the *only* thing that leaders should focus upon.

High-performing, values-aligned organizations balance the focus on *performance* as well as the *values* they want lived by team leaders and members every day. Employees in these companies deliver on performance promises and do so while demonstrating values of, for example, integrity, civility, and creativity.

Let's "take a drive" for a minute to learn more about the parts of an organizational constitution.

You're driving along a North American road and come to an intersection with a four-way stop. As you slow to a stop, you notice a car already stopped on your right. Do you go or do they go?

U.S. traffic rules say that the car arriving first has the right of way. Without hesitation, you wave the other driver on.

If you both had arrived at the intersection at the same time, you'd honor the traffic rule that says cars to the right have the right of way. Without hesitation, you'd wave the other driver on.

By knowing and aligning to traffic rules, drivers are able to get to where they need to go safely. No drama, no road rage—everyone simply "drives friendly" (as they say in Texas).

Traffic rules provide drivers with specific rights (the "right of way") and give drivers specific guidelines to follow in situations that might otherwise be ambiguous.

Your organization needs a similar set of rules to help leaders and employees understand how to be *great corporate citizens* as well as how to contribute to the organizations goals.

An organizational constitution answers the following questions:

- What are we trying to accomplish? (That's your organization's present-day *purpose*.)

- How are we expected to treat each other? (Those are your organization's *values* and *behaviors*.)

- What is our blueprint for going to market during this performance period? (That's your organization's *strategy*.)

- What performance targets will keep us on track, delivering what we've promised to our customers and stakeholders? (Those are your organization's *goals*.)

In most organizations, performance metrics are closely scrutinized with dashboards that frequently update (per hour, per shift, etc.). Performance management systems focus on goal planning, goal accomplishment, exceeding performance expectations, and the like.

Little else is consistently measured, monitored, or rewarded in most organizations.

If you measure, monitor, and reward only production, that's what people will focus on. They will get the results being monitored in any way they can—even through aggressive, "I win, you lose," approaches. Respectful treatment of each other and of customers may or may not happen.

THE PERFORMANCE-VALUES MATRIX

A model[4] may be helpful here. When Jack Welch was president of General Electric, he mandated that GE's values be equally as important as performance for everyone in the organization—leaders, managers, supervisors, and employees.

Welch was the first corporate leader on the planet to demand *both* performance and values from every organizational player, including himself.

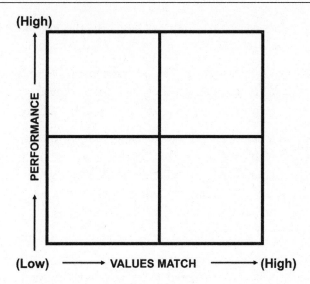

Figure 1.1 The Performance-Values Matrix
Source: The "Performance-Values Matrix" was originally published in the *"Gung Ho!"* *Participant Workbook*, Item #10832, © 2000 Blanchard Family Partnership and Ode to Joy Limited, and is included herein with the authors' permission.

The performance-values matrix outlines four possible combinations of performance and values. (See Figure 1.1.)

The vertical axis describes a player's performance at any point in time in the organization, with low performance on the bottom and high performance on the top.

The horizontal axis describes how well a player demonstrates the organization's espoused, desired values at any point in time, with low values match on the left and high values match on the right.

A caveat: Before one can apply this model to their team, department, or organization, clear performance expectations *and* clear values expectations must be defined and agreed to in advance by the organization's members.

The challenge with this model is how to measure the values match. Values must be as measurable as performance metrics and must be measured regularly (just as performance metrics are monitored).

The only way to shift values from lofty, vague references is to define values in *observable, tangible, measurable behaviors*.

Behaviors are measurable. Valued behaviors—the defined, specific behaviors that show alignment with your team or organization's desired values—are as measurable as performance targets and metrics.

Once performance and values expectations are clear, one can assess where any player fits in this matrix at any point in time. One simply assesses the degree to which a leader or employee is on the performance scale (missing, meeting, or exceeding performance expectations) and on the values scale (missing, meeting, or exceeding values expectations).

The best place for staff (leaders, managers, supervisors, and employees) to exist on this matrix is the upper-right quadrant. Players in that quadrant meet or exceed performance standards, and consistently demonstrate desired valued behaviors.

What should you do with high-performance, values-aligned players in your team or company? Trust them, honor them, validate them, compensate them, and, most importantly, *keep* them.

A not-so-good place for staff to reside in this matrix is the lower-left quadrant. "Lower-left" players fall short of performance expectations and do not consistently demonstrate desired valued behaviors.

What should you do with the low-performance, low-values player? *Lovingly set them free.* Or, as WD-40 Company president Garry Ridge says, "Share those employees with the competition!"

One could invest time and energy to raise these player's skills (to improve performance) and coach them to modify their interaction behaviors (to increase the values match), but research and experience show that such time does not pay off in the long run. It's best to let these folks go work somewhere else. "Lovingly" set them free, with dignity, because the way you treat staff—those that are leaving and those that are staying—says more about your values than any published statement.

Players in the bottom-right quadrant present an interesting challenge. What should you do with the values-led players who are unable to consistently perform? Train them, build skills, and even move them to different jobs that leverage their skills.

You don't want to lose the values match if you can help it. However, if these players are unable to consistently perform in any role, then you must lovingly set them free.

The upper-left quadrant is where the most damaging players reside. The high-performance, low-values match players are *poison* in your team or organization. They exceed performance expectations (which is good) while demonstrating a very different set of values than those you desire (which is not good, at all).

What must you do with these players? Lovingly set them free, as fast as you can. Their very existence in your team or organization erodes your leadership integrity and erodes trust among staff as well as customers.

An organizational constitution outlines your team's purpose, values, strategies, and goals. Holding all staff accountable for both performance and values ensures that your organization is populated by inspired, high-performing, values-aligned players.

THE COSTS OF MEASURING ONLY PERFORMANCE

What are the risks of *not* having defined values expectations—or of *not* managing to those desired valued behaviors?

Typically, when organizations don't have defined values or behaviors, leaders and employees treat each other (and even treat customers) badly because *no one is paying attention to values.* No one is measuring or monitoring the quality of interactions that happen daily.

In such work cultures, people can and will do *anything* to meet performance expectations—poach customers, overpromise to get the sale, stretch the truth to gain advantage, withhold information so a peer stumbles (or fails), withhold information so a customer makes the buy, and worse. Aggressive, self-serving behavior is the norm.

What is missing in these organizations is a clear definition of how "great corporate citizens" behave—and the commitment of all parties to

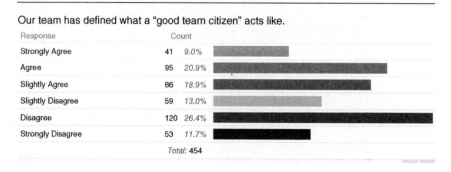

Our team has defined what a "good team citizen" acts like.

Response	Count		
Strongly Agree	41	9.0%	
Agree	95	20.9%	
Slightly Agree	86	18.9%	
Slightly Disagree	59	13.0%	
Disagree	120	26.4%	
Strongly Disagree	53	11.7%	
	Total: 454		

Figure 1.2   Good citizen responses from the Performance Values Assessment

demonstrate those behaviors. People need to understand exactly *how* people and customers must be treated in every interaction.

Look at Figure 1.2. It shows global responses to one of the survey questions from my Performance-Values Assessment.[5] The items in this assessment are ranked on a six-point scale. The two desirable answers are "strongly agree" and "agree." The other four answers are not desirable.

This particular item shows that slightly less than 30 percent of 454 global respondents strongly agree or agree that their team or company has defined what a "good team citizen" acts like. That means *just over 70 percent of respondents live in a work environment without behaviorally defined values.*

Figure 1.3 illustrates a similar item from another research project I have under way: the Great Boss Assessment.[6]

This leader has defined our team's constitution (purpose, values, strategies, and goals).

Response	Count		
Strongly Agree	29	10.7%	
Agree	72	26.6%	
Slightly Agree	60	22.1%	
Slightly Disagree	36	13.3%	
Disagree	48	17.7%	
Strongly Disagree	26	9.6%	
	Total: 271		

Figure 1.3   Defined values responses from the Great Boss Assessment

In this item, 38 percent of 271 global respondents believe their boss *has* defined their team's constitution (purpose, values, strategies, and goals). That degree of agreement is better than the "good team citizen" data above—but it still leaves *62 percent of respondents that live in a work culture without formally defined purpose, values, strategies, and goals.*

Let's look a bit more closely at Zappos, the online shoe and clothing retailer that is one of the most successful *and* values-aligned organizations on the planet today. Is Zappos a high-performing company? The data indicates that it is. The organization went from startup in 1999 with negligible sales to over $1 billion in gross sales in 2009. That's the same year Amazon purchased Zappos for $1.2 billion.

Zappos' wunderkind CEO, Tony Hsieh, gives much of the credit for the company's growth and success to their unique culture. Tony wanted Zappos to be a fun place to work with a family atmosphere that inspires workers.

He founded the company on ten formally defined values that employees embrace and make uniquely their own. Delivering happiness is what the company does for employees—and they, in turn, deliver happiness to Zappos customers.

Zappos employees see the culture there as an extended family, a club with a very deep sense of belonging to something special. Employees say they are accepted for who they are—they're not clones, they are unique teammates who trust and support each other. Zapponians (as they call themselves) feel treated like royalty—that's a powerful indication of workplace inspiration.

Amazon's CEO, Jeff Bezos, stated one thing very boldy when they purchased Zappos: Amazon would *not* change Zappos unique culture—they were operating beautifully and successfully. Amazon had no desire to change the culture there.

Zapponians publish a free culture book[7] every other year. Request your copy to learn how inspired and passionate Zappos team members are about their company, their culture, and their customers.

WD-40 Company is another benchmark global organization with top performance and significant values alignment. President and

CEO Garry Ridge says, "Values are the written reminder of the only acceptable behaviors in our organization."

One of WD-40 Company's values is "do the right thing." Ridge says this value inspires conversations every day that challenge plans, decisions, and actions to ensure the "right thing" happens for customers.

Another WD-40 Company value is "accountability." Every WD-40 Company tribe member makes a pledge, "I am responsible for taking action, asking questions, getting answers, and making decisions. I won't wait for someone to tell me. If I need to know, I'm responsible for asking. I have no right to be offended that I didn't 'get this sooner.' If I'm doing something others should know about, I'm responsible for telling them."

Garry believes "with rights comes responsibility." Personal responsibility comes first, and accountability for performance and for values naturally occurs in the WD-40 Company culture.

If a player doesn't demonstrate personal responsibility for performance and values at WD-40 Company, they simply can't work there anymore.

We'll learn more from Garry about the WD-40 Company "tribe's" culture journey and values in my interview with him in Chapter 6.

Both Zappos and WD-40 Company are WorldBlu "Democratic Workplace"[8] multi-year award winners. WorldBlu is an organization that promotes workplace inspiration in their 10 Principles of Organizational Democracy, which emphasizes organizational cultures based on freedom, not fear and control.

Unfortunately, workplace inspiration does not happen naturally—it happens only by intention. It requires clear standards, modeling, constant tending, alignment efforts, and celebration of traction towards a high-performing, values-aligned culture.

To be effective and actionable, an organizational constitution must include formal statements of organizational purpose, values, strategy, and goals.

Of these elements, most (not all) companies are familiar with purpose statements, strategic plans, and clear goals. The element that organizations have the least amount of experience developing is values—more specifically, *valued behaviors that are observable, tangible, and measurable.*

Values are the foundation of great corporate citizenship and of workplace inspiration. Only when values are defined in observable, tangible, and measurable terms can they drive desired behaviors every day.

Let's look at a value that is desired by many organizations around the globe: integrity.

How would you define integrity for your company or team? What do you mean by integrity in your workplace? Note a phrase or sentence that describes what you mean by integrity. If your team or company has an integrity value defined, feel free to use that definition here:

_____

_____

_____

_____

_____

Now, consider how you'd like people to *demonstrate* integrity, as you've defined it. How would they be acting so that, when you observe them, you'd see they were honoring your integrity value?

Note two or three behaviors that fit your integrity definition:

_____

_____

_____

_____

_____

How, though, might team members define integrity? Would they have different behaviors in mind as they consider how they and peers would model their definition of integrity?

It is quite likely that they would. Ask 20 people in your organization what integrity looks like, and you'll likely get 20 different answers. You might even get 30 different answers.

You see the problem. Everyone has a slightly different version of the value and of the behaviors in mind, and everyone judges others on how well leaders and peers demonstrate *their* version.

An organizational constitution creates *common* agreements based on *shared* purpose and values. These "rules of engagement" are formalized so every leader and employee knows what values expectations are—and can model them, praise them, coach to them, and redirect misaligned behaviors.

Defining values and behaviors and then holding everyone in the company or team accountable for living them creates continuity and sanity. Every player knows what's expected of him or her.

Valued behaviors are *liberating rules* for every leader and employee—they describe exactly what's expected. Players don't have to spend time hedging or guessing how one should treat others or be treated. There is no more toleration of rude behavior or workplace bullying.

Compare your "integrity" notes to how one client outlined its "integrity" value:

Value: Integrity

Definition: We are accountable for our actions. We do what we say we will do. We do not compromise our organization's values, no matter what.

Behaviors:

- I hold myself accountable for my commitments and actions; I keep my promises.
- I attack problems and processes, not people.
- I accept responsibility and apologize if I jeopardize respect or trust.
- I align all of my plans, decisions, and actions with the organization's purpose and values.

These behaviors are in the form of "I" statements. They describe how every employee, no matter their title, role, or responsibilities, behaves, day to day.

These behaviors are *positively* described; they outline how you want people to *act* daily. The behaviors don't say "I will . . ." because "will" means I *might* do it later. I don't have to do it *now*. You want every player to *do* these behaviors *now*, consistently, always.

These behaviors outline what you want members of the organization to *do* daily (not what you *don't* want them to do). This lets every leader and employee know how they are expected to behave in order to demonstrate the organization's integrity value.

Let me offer a brief lesson about the power of "do" messages. The human brain processes "do" messages more quickly and efficiently than "don't" messages. A couple of examples highlight the importance of stating desired behavior in positive terms.

Let's say you are riding your bike on a narrow trail. If you tell yourself, "Don't fall!" your brain hears, "Fall!" You lose focus, you lose desired straight-line tracking and momentum, and you fall. Ouch.

Or, you are playing golf with friends. You find yourself on the tee box with your driver in hand. A nice, green, mowed, expansive fairway lies before you. There is a lake along the left side of the fairway. As you line up your shot, you say to yourself, "Don't hit it into the lake!" Your brain hears, "Hit it into the lake!" You lose focus, and—despite your best intentions—your ball goes right into the lake with a splash.

"Don't" messages are used quite often in the work environment (and at home, for that matter). Workplace "don't" messages include such statements as "Don't be late" (for meetings or project deadlines), "Don't be a jerk" (don't yell or be rude), "Don't promise what you can't deliver," and the like.

By stating messages in *positive* terms and stating desired behaviors ("do" messages), more consistent and frequent alignment to that behavior occurs. By stating, "Be on time," "Be kind," or "Be of service," these messages become much more actionable.

Valued behaviors become the metrics for great corporate citizenship and for workplace inspiration. Once these valued behaviors are published, leaders must live them and coach them consistently.

Leaders must then create systems (like a custom values survey) that measure how well leaders and employees demonstrate these behaviors day to day.

We'll learn about how to measure values alignment in Chapter 7. The results of a leader or employee's custom values survey profile can be combined with their performance appraisal to provide a more complete picture of that leader or employee's contributions to the organization.

How Does an Organizational Constitution Help Your Company, Department, or Team?

You can't afford to operate without an organizational constitution. The costs of leaving your team or organization's culture to chance are too great.

The positive financial impact of aligning plans, decisions, and actions to clear purpose, values, and behaviors is impressive and the benefits undeniable.

One of the first noticeable changes in the work environments of our culture clients is the growth in employee engagement. In morale surveys, satisfaction surveys, and engagement surveys, our culture clients have seen 35–40 percent engagement gains in 12 to 18 months.

What is the benefit to organizations of greater employee engagement? Let's look at the research.

In its 2013 "State of the American Workplace" report,[9] Gallup, Inc. describes how engaged workers help their organizations succeed. Engaged workers have significantly higher productivity, profitability, and customer ratings, less turnover and absenteeism, and fewer safety incidents than their disengaged colleagues.

However, Gallup's research indicates that only 30 percent of American workers are engaged, leaving more than two-thirds of workplace populations not engaged or actively disengaged.

Gallup estimates that actively disengaged workers cost U.S. businesses more than $450 billion in lost productivity each year.

In a 2006 study[10] of more than 23,000 business units, Gallup found that units in the top 25 percent of employee engagement scores generated 12 percent higher productivity than units in the bottom 25 percent of employee engagement scores.

Kenexa's 2008 study[11] of 64 organizations found that companies with highly engaged employees achieve twice the annual net income of companies whose employees are less than highly engaged.

Gallup's 2010 "State of the Global Workplace" report[12] found that most countries studied have fewer engaged workers than in U.S. workplaces. Only Brazil, Costa Rica, Guatemala, and Bahrain were close to the U.S. engagement totals.

In his book, *The Integrity Dividend*,[13] Dr. Tony Simons describes the benefits of what he calls "behavioral integrity." Simons defines behavioral integrity as managers demonstrating their organization's values and doing what they say they will do (keep their commitments).

Simon's found that when employees believe their bosses have behavioral integrity, employee commitment goes up. Committed employees apply discretionary energy in service to the organization's goals and customers. Customers notice and appreciate employee's discretionary energy, and support the company by buying and promoting its products and services.

The net gain: Profits grew 2.5 percent for every one-quarter point bump on a 10-point behavioral integrity scale.

For one of Simons' clients, a hotel chain, every one-quarter point bump earned each hotel $250,000 net profit. This was free money, generated entirely by employee perceptions of their boss's behavioral integrity.

Here are a few more examples that demonstrate the positive impact of employee engagement on business outcomes and customer service rankings:

- Morrison Management Specialists increased client satisfaction by 1 percentage point for every 2 percentage point increase in employee engagement.[14]

- Fabick CAT, a Caterpillar dealer in southern Missouri, USA, improved "percent of industry net sales" by 300 percent.[15]

- Highly engaged employees were 87 percent less likely to leave their companies than their disengaged counterparts.[16]

- MolsonCoors found that engaged employees were five times less likely than nonengaged employees to have a safety incident and seven times less likely to have a lost-time safety incident.[17]

High-performing, values-aligned companies report higher levels of employee well being than companies that do not ensure values-alignment. Research reported on the Positivity Works[18] website shows that employees with high well being:

- Deliver 31 percent higher productivity than employees with low well being.[19]

- Demonstrate three times higher creativity on the job.[20]

- Generate 37 percent higher sales results.[21]

- Report being 10 times more engaged by their jobs.[22]

- Report being three times more satisfied with their jobs.[23]

CLIENT IMPACT

Global research results universally prove that engaged employees generate greater profits and better customer experiences. What about clients that have used our "organizational constitution" process—what do their results show?

One client came to us because of low employee engagement survey scores. They scored 32 out of 100 possible points, the worst scores of the 8 business units owned by their corporate parent. This plant's senior leadership team embraced our culture process fully and promptly.

They defined values with observable behaviors so everyone—leaders and employees—understood what the rules were for effective daily interactions. They increased performance accountability across their production lines. They measured how well leaders lived the organization's new valued behaviors. They praised leaders who modeled their values, coached leaders who struggled, and redirected leaders who didn't model or manage to the new values.

Within six months, conflicts, absenteeism, rework, and grievances dropped by 60 percent. Efficiency improved. Customers reported amazement at the "new service attitude" that company staff displayed.

When the next employee engagement survey came around twelve months later, their plant scored 62 out of 100 points! Theirs was the biggest gain in engagement scores of any of business unit in their company system, and, theirs was the top score across the organization.

At the 18-month mark, employee engagement had grown 45 percent, customer service rankings had grown 45 percent, and *profits had grown 35 percent.*

Plant leaders gave all the credit to every leader and employee's alignment to their organizational constitution.

Another client, a seven-state region of a large retailer, embraced our culture change process because the new senior leader's vision wasn't taking hold fast enough.

Joel, the region's senior leader, believed and preached "People with Passion drive Performance!" Joel's messaging and coaching in his first 18 months in the position helped *some* store managers "get it." However, most store managers did not.

Twelve months after creating their organizational constitution and managing to it (with our guidance), Joel's region enjoyed 40 percent gains in employee engagement, 40 percent gains in the customer experience, and 30 percent gains in profits.

A manufacturing plant in the Midwestern United States discovered a fabulous peripheral benefit to their organizational constitution. Their small town suffered flash flooding one spring, which caused tremendous damage in their community. Families were evacuated with little time to gather for necessities.

Plant employees banded together to provide food, clothing, and transportation for their neighbors. They volunteered hundreds of hours for the Red Cross at the evacuation center. They secured funds from the plant's parent company to rebuild homes and businesses in the following months.

The plant manager said in the 40 years the plant had been operating in that town, no one had ever seen employees rally so quickly and confidently to serve their fellow community members. Some of the employees who volunteered to help had also suffered significant losses in the flooding. "Our values and behaviors didn't just apply inside the plant. These employees made sure they applied in our town, too," she said.

Most clients don't see these engagement, service, and profit gains quite so quickly—it usually takes 18 to 24 months to align expectations and practices to your unique organizational constitution. However, *these* leaders—and their organization members—embraced their purpose, values, and behaviors at exactly the right time. These leaders and employees were ready, even primed, for the disruptive technology of an organizational constitution.

The moral of the story: If you're only paying attention to results, you're leaving money on the table.

YOUR LEADERSHIP LEGACY

Let's discuss one more beneficial impact to creating and managing to an organizational constitution: your leadership legacy.

You create your legacy with every plan, decision, and action. Everything you do tells your boss, peers, team members, and customers what you stand for.

What you value is transparent through your actions.

For many leaders, legacy isn't something they are conscious about. They are conscious—and intentional—about getting stuff done, getting products out the door, getting services delivered as promised. "Legacy?" one leaders asked me. "I'm not thinking about my leadership legacy. I'm just trying to keep the doors open and make more money today than we spend!"

I understand the need for leaders to manage output; those are promises that must be kept. And, if your work environment isn't consistently safe, inspiring, and respectful, that environment erodes every employee's willingness to engage in the work, and it erodes every employee's personal well being.

That's *not* something to be proud of.

And, it costs you money: hard dollars . . . in opportunity lost, in mistakes tolerated, in "if they don't love or trust me, I won't love or trust them," lousy efforts by team members, and more.

This could be the legacy you're leaving, right now.

Yet every one of us has had great bosses that inspired us, who brought out our best, who treated us like royalty.

When I ask leaders what their best bosses did to deserve that coveted title, they consistently report these "great boss" behaviors:

- He trusted and respected me.
- She had high standards of me.
- He listened to my ideas.
- She supported me, even when things weren't going perfectly.
- When I made a mistake, he asked me about it, promptly and respectfully. He let me know he was disappointed and needed my best, every moment.
- She never blamed me—she knew I was doing my best.

We *know* what a positive leadership legacy requires; we've seen it and experienced it.

The hectic pace and incredible demands of our jobs have simply taken our eyes off the prize.

A few additional items from my research will shed light on the need for a positive leadership legacy. Figure 1.4 shows global responses to another survey item from my Great Boss Assessment.[24]

This leader inspires my best efforts each day.

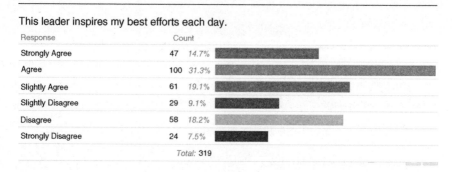

Response	Count		
Strongly Agree	47	14.7%	
Agree	100	31.3%	
Slightly Agree	61	19.1%	
Slightly Disagree	29	9.1%	
Disagree	58	18.2%	
Strongly Disagree	24	7.5%	

Total: 319

Figure 1.4   Inspiration responses from the Great Boss Assessment

Forty-six percent of respondents strongly agree or agree (again, these are the two desirable ratings) that their boss inspires their best efforts each day. That's not bad—but it means that *54 percent of respondents work for bosses who do* not *inspire their best efforts.*

Figure 1.5 shows an additional legacy-related item from the Great Boss Assessment. This item gauges agreement on the degree to which respondents see their leader "coaching team members on behaviors that erode team performance, trust, or respect." Just under 37 percent believe their leader does; that means 63 percent experience a work environment where leaders do not address such behaviors.

One final legacy-related item from the Great Boss Assessment is shown in Figure 1.6. This item asks respondents to rate how quickly their leader addresses team issues. Slightly less than 36 percent believe

This leader "calls us on our crap," coaching team members on behaviors that erode performance, trust, or respect.

Response	Count		
Strongly Agree	17	6.3%	
Agree	82	30.3%	
Slightly Agree	59	21.8%	
Slightly Disagree	50	18.5%	
Disagree	43	15.9%	
Strongly Disagree	20	7.4%	

Total: 271

Figure 1.5   Coaching responses from the Great Boss Assessment

This leader doesn't let team issues fester. S/he promptly facilitates team problem solving to address issues.

Response	Count	
Strongly Agree	24 8.9%	
Agree	72 26.6%	
Slightly Agree	53 19.6%	
Slightly Disagree	48 17.7%	
Disagree	45 16.6%	
Strongly Disagree	29 10.7%	
	Total: 271	

Figure 1.6   Team responses from the Great Boss Assessment

their boss doesn't let team issues fester. That means that *73 percent believe their boss lets team issues fester.*

There is no time like the present to build a stronger, positive leadership legacy. You may as well—you're going to be there in the foreseeable future anyway, right?

This book aims to educate readers that effective leadership involves much more than managing output. With an organizational constitution, the framework for a safe, inspiring, *fun*, and productive work environment is clear.

With an organizational constitution, consistent workplace inspiration is within reach.

Ready to learn more? The next chapter will help you get clearer about *your* purpose, values, and leadership philosophy. Then we'll dive into defining your team or company's organizational constitution: purpose, values and behaviors, strategies and goals.

CHAPTER 2

It Starts with You

I'm delighted you have decided to learn more about creating an organizational constitution for your team or company and managing alignment to it daily.

You've learned that leaders are in charge of an organization's culture. Refining or tweaking your team's or company's current culture means that you will be the banner carrier for your organizational constitution.

You are ready to embrace the leader's responsibility to be a proactive champion of your desired culture.

The demands of proactive culture refinement are significant. You'll need to invest time and energy communicating, modeling, and reinforcing your desired culture. You can't delegate primary responsibility for this—this job is yours.

You'll need to embrace servant leadership in daily interactions.

You'll need to promptly and genuinely praise and encourage aligned efforts by team members and teams.

Since there are only 24 hours in a day (I checked Google—it's true), you'll not be able to simply *add* these activities to your daily workload. You'll need to redirect time and energy to culture-champion activities from less important activities.

The credibility of the culture refinement will rely on the degree to which you, as the culture champion, are consistently modeling the desired values and behaviors.

When you begin the culture refinement journey with your team or company and define different expectations (values and behaviors, particularly), scrutiny of your every plan, decision, and action will increase tenfold. You'll be under a microscope, in and out of the workplace.

You must live and breathe the values and behaviors you publish as part of the organizational constitution. They apply to you inside and outside the workplace. They are your personal values engine.

Any misstep on your part will be construed as "See? I told you. This is just another flavor of the month. The boss (or company) isn't really serious about this culture stuff."

Letting a team leader get away with cursing out a team member? That will generate a negative buzz: "How come the boss didn't come down on Larry for losing his temper with Angela? That's against our values—but nothing happened!"

If you cut in line at the grocery store express lane when you're in a hurry, what message does that send? That will be seen as proof that the values and behaviors aren't really important to you.

If you drive through a yellow light at an intersection in your community, what message does that send? It's another indicator that the culture thing is just a passing fad—and that you are not serious about the values and behaviors you've defined.

This scrutiny is unfair, yet it is completely understandable. And it is inevitable. You need to expect it and live up to it.

Most team leaders and team members have never lived in an intentional, high-performance, values-aligned work environment. They don't know exactly how it's going to work. They don't know what's expected of them.

Just as with any change, those humans would rather not go down an unknown path; they'd rather stay in the known (even if the known work environment isn't fun to live in!).

You will be the face of this culture refinement.

As we've discussed, managing to your organizational constitution is a long-term initiative. Think of proactive culture management as a huge, important, ongoing project. It'll take time and focus and energy to keep the project on track.

Unlike most projects, this culture initiative will never be finished. You'll see terrific alignment in the first 18 to 24 months, but your work environment is always evolving.

New team leaders are hired—and must embrace your organizational constitution. New team members are brought on board—and must embrace your organizational constitution.

New markets or products can create stresses that can easily pull people away from values alignment.

If your organization falls behind in your budget, those stresses can easily pull people away from values alignment.

Workplace inspiration is fragile. Creating a safe, inspiring, fun, productive work environment takes tending, observation, checking in, redirecting, coaching, and so on every day.

You must understand these demands and requirements, and embark on this journey with your eyes wide open.

You must understand *who you are as a person*—and create a strong foundation for yourself as culture champion of your team or company.

Clarity breeds confidence that inspires commitment and competence. Culture champions must be *intentional*—not casual—with their own personal constitution (purpose, values and behaviors, and leadership philosophy).

Every person on the planet has a purpose he or she is acting upon. All people have values they act upon. They have behaviors they demonstrate. They even have a leadership or influencing philosophy they act upon.

Each person's purpose, values, behaviors, and philosophy may not be at all formalized, but they still drive daily plans, decisions, and actions, nonetheless.

The problem is that we can tweak our version of our purpose or values or behavior or philosophy day in and day out to serve ourselves better. These tweaks, though, erode consistency and inhibit the creation of a strong service foundation.

The most effective culture champions are very specific about their beliefs. They formalize them and share them so that others can give them feedback about how well they're living their beliefs.

We'll not be casual about your personal constitution—we'll be intentional!

This chapter provides the best practices of effective culture champions and gives you proven tools to help you embrace those best practices.

This chapter's Culture Effectiveness Assessment ranks the degree to which you, as a team or company leader, have clarified your own purpose, values, behaviors, and leadership philosophy, have shared them with your team, and invite feedback on your alignment to your constitution.

Culture Effectiveness Assessment #2: Personal Purpose, Values, and Philosophy	Strongly Disagree	Disagree	Slightly Disagree	Slightly Agree	Agree	Strongly Agree
1. Clarity of Personal Purpose My purpose statement succinctly describes my reason for being on this planet.	1	2	3	4	5	6
2. Clarity of Personal Values My values statement includes formal definitions of the principles I choose to live by in every interaction, every day.	1	2	3	4	5	6
3. My Values Are Measurable My values are defined in specific, tangible, and measurable behaviors.	1	2	3	4	5	6
4. Clarity of Leadership Philosophy I have formalized my leadership philosophy, which outlines my beliefs about leadership, whom I	1	2	3	4	5	6

Culture Effectiveness Assessment #2: Personal Purpose, Values, and Philosophy	Strongly Disagree	Disagree	Slightly Disagree	Slightly Agree	Agree	Strongly Agree
serve, what outcomes we build together, and what people can expect from me. My leadership philosophy is based on servant leadership in action.						
5. I Ask for Feedback on My Purpose, Values, and Leadership Philosophy I share my personal purpose, values, behaviors, and leadership philosophy with my direct reports. I ask for their feedback regularly to gauge how well I'm living my personal constitution.	1	2	3	4	5	6

Let's build your culture champion personal constitution. We'll start with your personal purpose and values, and then move on to your leadership philosophy.

CLARIFY YOUR PERSONAL PURPOSE

All sustainable, meaningful work begins with a solid foundation. The first piece of this foundation is your positive personal purpose statement.

If you've done work on a personal mission statement or values clarification in the past, this process will feel comfortable to you. You'll be able to leverage the work you've already done, refining your personal purpose to ensure its relevance for this culture journey.

For most of you, this will be a new path. These instructions will walk you step-by-step through a proven process to formalize your personal purpose (and values, in the next section).

We'll be looking at your *life* purpose and values, not just a set for your *workplace*. Our core purpose and values don't change based on the roles we choose. They remain the same, a solid foundation for whatever we're doing.

Let's get started with defining your life purpose. Your life purpose should clearly and succinctly describe what talents you offer, whom you will serve, and what you are striving for: to what desirable end you are working.

We'll focus on a *personal purpose based on service to others*, giving of ourselves so that others benefit, grow, and develop.

You could certainly develop a self-centered purpose statement. We all know people who live their lives exclusively for their own selfish desires. However, *culture championing requires a servant leadership heart, mind, and spirit*. We'll set you up for success with a purpose statement grounded in service to others.

Let's use my current draft personal purpose statement as an example. I say "current draft" because I refine this statement about once a year. I find that I'm learning and growing constantly—and insights from my ongoing development need to be reflected in my purpose statement so I can ensure I'm on track with my developing self.

Here is my current personal purpose statement:

To use my expertise and passion to inspire and encourage leaders to clarify their personal values and to create workplace inspiration.

What talents am I choosing to leverage? I've chosen my expertise and my passion as the most relevant skill sets for my life purpose.

Whom am I focused on serving? What is the specific population I'm trying to impact? My chosen population is leaders, people with influencing responsibility in teams, departments, divisions, and companies around the globe.

What am I striving for? To what end am I working? I want those leaders to clarify their core principles—their personal values—and to create and sustain workplace inspiration for those around them.

Though I'm using a template approach with the "talent, focus, and striving for" elements of personal purpose, my statement is a positive and accurate statement of my personal reason for being on this earth.

Feel free to use my statement as a template for yours.

Start building your personal purpose statement by answering the following questions in the spaces provided.

1. **What are your core talents?** What of your many skills and areas of expertise can be leveraged to the greater good of those around you? Examples might include authentic listening, teaching, solving problems, and the like.

   _____

   _____

   _____

   _____

2. **Whom are you focused on serving?** What is the specific population you're trying to impact? It could be neighbors, direct reports, members of your department, students, or others. Be as specific as possible. Too broad a population ("members of the human race") will make your impact difficult to gauge.

   _____

   _____

   _____

   _____

3. **What are you striving for?** What is the desired beneficial impact of your applied talents on your selected population? (These are harder questions to answer than the previous ones. These answers can move you from right answers—*I'm good at X*—toward better answers—*I'm able to consistently inspire X*.)

   _____

   _____

   _____

   _____

Now, pull the most compelling, impactful answers from each of the three previous questions into a single purpose statement that clearly describes your personal life purpose.

_____

_____

_____

_____

Realize that this initial step will take a bit of time, a bit of wordsmithing, and a bit of testing. Once you've drafted your purpose statement, share it with people you trust—family, friends, or coworkers. Ask them if it rings true, based on what they know of you. Listen and refine.

CLARIFY YOUR PERSONAL VALUES AND ALIGNED BEHAVIORS

Next, formalize the values that characterize you at your best. When you're at your best, you easily live the principles that you hold most dear naturally and consistently.

This section will help you identify the values that you would like to be known for and that guide your most aligned plans, decisions, and actions every day.

And this section will help you identify the behaviors that, when you demonstrate them, indicate you're acting in alignment with your personal values.

We'll follow this format for your personal values and behaviors:

- **Value.** What word or phrase specifies the value you want to demonstrate?

- **Definition.** What exactly do you mean by that word or phrase? Define it crisply and succinctly so you understand what you mean by that principle.

- **Behaviors.** How will you model this value? Specify *no more than four* observable, tangible, measurable behaviors that you must demonstrate to keep to this value daily. Why no more than four? Keep it simple. We humans can remember lists of 3 to 4 items pretty easily. Lists of 10 or more are much more difficult to keep "top of mind" and actionable.

It might be helpful to look at an example. My values and definitions follow. Note that your values list might be much different than mine.

- **Integrity.** I do what I say I will do, keep my commitments, and act on my values, so I may hold my head high at the end of each day.

- **Learning.** I scan the environment for current research and discoveries that can enlighten my colleagues, my clients, and me.

- **Joy.** I celebrate the pleasure derived from doing work I'm good at and enjoy with interesting, willing learners, and bask in the core grace I feel when helping others grow.

- **Perfection.** I deliver what I promise so that objectives are exceeded, clients and partners are wowed, and I continuously sharpen the saw so future results are better than today's.

Let's start. Think about the values or principles that you'd be proud to be known for. List them here:

_____

_____

_____

_____

Add to this list any additional values you would like to demonstrate consistently in your life and work. Borrow from my values list, and consider these additional values.

Abundance	Freedom	Nobility	Service
Agility	Fun	Outrageousness	Significance
Audacity	Generosity	Passion	Stability
Brilliance	Harmony	Philanthropy	Teamwork
Creativity	Humility	Poise	Trust
Dream	Integrity	Proactivity	Valor
Excellence	Learning	Responsiveness	Wonder

Finally, think of people you highly respect, people you love to engage with. What values do they espouse and demonstrate? List those as well, as one or two might fit perfectly in your personal values list.

Now pull together your preferred values list. Identify three to five values you'd like to model in daily interactions at home, in the community, and at work—and note them here:

_____

_____

_____

_____

Why three to five values? Why not 10? Again, you're trying to create *clarity* about values and *alignment* to behaviors. Too long a list of values or behaviors creates confusion, not confidence.

By limiting your values to three to five, you'll find greater appreciation, comprehension, and behavioral alignment toward your best self, every day.

DEFINE YOUR VALUES

Next you must define your values so that there is no question in your or anyone's mind about what you *exactly* mean by the values you desire to live by.

By formalizing what your values mean to you, you are not only clearing the right path through our daily jungle, you are shining intense, clear light on that desired path.

In the absence of clear values definitions, your head, heart, and hands will work harder to figure out the right principles to model each day. With clear definitions, you move forward with clarity and confidence in these principles.

Let's say one of your values is excellence. If you assume that, "I don't have to define this value. Everyone knows what excellence means," you'll be unpleasantly surprised a lot of the time.

One player might assume excellence means that you will do your tasks perfectly, every time. Another might assume that excellence means you will teach her how to do her tasks perfectly.

Another might believe excellence means you will delegate authority and responsibility to them promptly so they can act independently on every task.

Yet another player might assume excellence means that you will approve expenditures to get the best equipment and the best raw materials and the best skilled employees possible to ensure goals are met.

If each of these players judges you on *their* definition of excellence, they'll: 1) be disappointed in you because you're not aligned with their personal definition, and 2) complain to their peers at how badly you live your excellence value.

This is a recipe for confusion, frustration, and conflict.

A clear, succinct values definition helps people that interact with you daily by knowing what you mean by each of your values.

Define each of your values in *desirable* terms—say what it *is*, not what it isn't. You don't need to give examples—those we'll cover with your specific valued behaviors for each defined value.

To build your knowledge base of personal values and definitions, let's look at a few more examples from some of my clients.

Value: Health

Definition: I treat my body, mind, and spirit with respect so I can serve my purpose without distraction for as long as possible.

Value: Peace

Definition: I engage others kindly and respectfully. I debate ideas while honoring people. Where there is discontent, I learn how to help reduce its presence.

Value: Nobility

Definition: I hold every person in high regard. I see each person I engage with as capable of great accomplishments and great ideas, and build avenues for them to achieve their best selves.

Value: Service

Definition: Service to others is the highest calling on this earth. My responsibility is to smooth the path for my own unselfish service and for others to serve equally well.

Feel free to use these examples as templates for your personal values definitions.

Let's get rolling! List your top three to five personal values and add definitions for each value in the space provided:

Value: _____

Definition: _____

_____

_____

Value: _____

Definition: _____

_____

_____

Value: _____

Definition: _____

_____

_____

Value: _____

Definition: _____

_____

_____

Value: _____

Definition: _____

_____

_____

ADD OBSERVABLE, TANGIBLE, MEASURABLE BEHAVIORS TO EACH VALUE

This next important step in crafting your personal values is adding behavioral examples to each value.

I call these "valued behaviors," which describe exactly how you want to interact with people in life and at work every day.

These behaviors define your playing field for great personal citizenship.

Here are a few more examples from clients to build up your valued behaviors knowledge base.

Value: Love

Behaviors:

- I am compassionate toward people I interact with.
- I express gratitude for people's efforts and accomplishments.
- I expect the best and give people the benefit of the doubt.

Value: Respect

Behaviors:

- I treat others, at all times, with dignity and respect.

- I do not blame. I look for ways to solve problems and learn so we don't make the same mistakes again.
- I do not use crude language, act rudely, or discount anyone I work with—bosses, peers, or customers.

Value: Contribution

Behaviors:

- I keep my promises.
- I "sharpen the saw" regularly, boosting my skill sets to ensure I exceed performance standards.
- I help my team and team members succeed by offering help when it's needed.

Value: Philanthropy

Behaviors:

- I actively participate in our annual charity campaign, generating at least $5,000 in annual giving from others and myself.
- I volunteer at least five hours a month at the charity of my choice.
- I formally pay it forward at least once a month, through layaway angels or similar programs in my community.

We'll start identifying your valued behaviors by brainstorming potential behaviors for each value. In the spaces following, note behaviors that you'd be proud to demonstrate while you're modeling this value.

I use the term "demonstrate" intentionally. As noted earlier, you cannot measure nor hold people accountable for what they "think," what their "attitude" is, or what they "believe." You can, however, measure and hold yourself (and others) accountable for demonstrating—acting on—clearly defined valued behaviors.

Note down six to eight potential aligned behaviors for each of your values.

Value:_____

Behaviors:

- _____

- _____

- _____

Value:_____

Behaviors:

- _____

- _____

- _____

Value:_____

Behaviors:

- _____

- _____

- _____

Value:_____

Behaviors:

- _____

- _____

- _____

Value:_____

Behaviors:

- _____

- _____

- _____

Next, cull through the behaviors you've noted to reduce the list to three to four behaviors per value. Really, identify at least three but no more than four valued behaviors (simplify, simplify, simplify).

These questions may help with your selection process. For behaviors you're considering, ask yourself:

- **Is this an observable behavior?** Can I assess my demonstration of this behavior by asking people I work with to watch and/or listen to my interactions with customers, peers, or stakeholders? If not, toss it or refine it.

- **Is this behavior measurable?** Can I be reliably "scored" on this behavior, asking people I work with regularly to assess my demonstration of this behavior? Can others rank the degree to which I model or demonstrate this behavior on a scale of low to moderate to high at any point in time? If not, toss it or refine it.

YOUR VALUES, DEFINITIONS, AND BEHAVIORS

Now, pull these important elements together. This pivotal piece of your personal constitution defines how you intend to behave in daily interactions.

This piece outlines what great personal citizenship looks, acts, and sounds like from you, every day.

Rewrite your values and definitions first. The rewriting might cause you to do some slight wordsmithing that will clarify the meaning of your values.

The rewriting takes a little extra time, but it will help build clarity in your mind, which is critically important.

Then, add your identified three to four valued behaviors, ensuring they outline tangible, observable, measurable behaviors for each value.

Value: _____

Definition: _____

_____

_____

Behaviors:

- _____
- _____
- _____
- _____

Value: _____

Definition: _____

_____

_____

Behaviors:

- _____
- _____
- _____
- _____

Value: _____

Definition: _____

_____

_____

Behaviors:

- _____
- _____
- _____
- _____

Value: _____

Definition: _____

_____

_____

Behaviors:

- _____
- _____
- _____
- _____

Value: _____

Definition: _____

_____

_____

Behaviors:

- _____
- _____
- _____
- _____

Great work! You've got a solid draft of your personal values, definitions, and valued behaviors.

As with your purpose statement draft, your efforts with your draft values, definitions, and behaviors are just beginning. Next you must socialize these ideas, sharing them with peers, bosses, and team members. They may have clarifying questions that may prompt more wordsmithing of your statement.

And, you'll invite them to help you stay on track with your personal constitution.

FORMALIZE YOUR LEADERSHIP PHILOSOPHY

The last piece of your personal constitution is your leadership philosophy. Your leadership philosophy is a statement of your beliefs about leading others, your intentions when leading others, and what others can expect of you in your leadership capacity.

What are your beliefs about leading and motivating people? These beliefs will flow naturally from reflection about the people who have influenced you in your past and from your purpose and values.

If, for example, you believe that "ordinary people can accomplish extraordinary things when goals are clear and leaders serve followers' needs," that might be a foundational element of your leadership philosophy.

The vital question to have in mind as you craft your leadership philosophy is, "Are you a servant leader or a self-serving leader?"

You can't be "kind of" a servant leader any more than you can be "kind of" a self-serving leader! You'll be one or the other. If you've clarified your purpose, values, and beliefs, our research indicates that you'll model servant leadership more consistently and frequently.

We'll talk about servant leadership in more detail at the end of this chapter.

Let's look at the leadership philosophy proposed by one of my clients. I've been working with this organization's senior leaders on culture refinement for three years. At this stage, they've asked me to bring servant leadership into their organization's work environment. The timing of this effort is perfect, as there are a lot of really positive culture elements in place in this company.

And, they want to take the vital step to ensure all leaders are serving team members, every minute of every day.

Their senior leadership team formalized a company-wide leadership philosophy. This service mind-set is one they want all company leaders to embrace. It states:

> Our leaders demonstrate courage, confidence, and commitment while connecting with and inspiring others to achieve extraordinary results through teamwork.

Creating an organizational leadership philosophy is a great place for this team to start. However, dear reader, you may not be in charge of a big organization. Your sphere of influence might be a team or department or division.

We'll use this sample statement to help you define your personal leadership philosophy. We'll then outline how you can best share that philosophy, inviting feedback as you attempt to live that philosophy in daily interactions.

There are benefits of formalizing and then publishing your personal leadership philosophy:

- It *makes a promise* that you are then committed to deliver on. You, the leader, understand the minimum standard you are expected to meet with your leadership efforts.

- You can reflect daily on your plans, decisions, and actions to *gauge how well you are living up to your leadership philosophy*. A proactive part of this reflection would include engaging key players (direct or indirect reports) in conversations about how they perceive your plans, decisions, and actions.

An effective leadership philosophy is different than your personal purpose, values, and valued behaviors. While your leadership philosophy will be built upon the *foundation* your clear personal purpose and values statement creates, it is specific to your leadership intentions and efforts in the workplace, in a community organization (wherever you are taking a leadership role).

Let's define an effective personal leadership philosophy as a values-aligned statement that helps you inspire consistent high performance and authentic positive relationships with each of your team members, every day.

Your leadership philosophy outlines your beliefs about leadership, what a great leader does, and what people can expect from you in day-to-day interactions.

Your leadership philosophy sets the context for your influencing efforts and sets a high standard for your own values alignment as you craft workplace inspiration through an organizational constitution.

Here's a great example from Mark Deterding,[1] an inspiring culture champion, a proven business executive, and a successful leadership coach and consultant. Mark's personal leadership philosophy is a bit more detailed than the sample noted earlier. His leadership philosophy:

> I believe in being a humble servant leader who is absolutely persistent on driving improvement. I ensure clarity of purpose and vision and then create an environment that allows for that vision to be effectively carried out. I do this by clear communication, and empowering and developing people to allow them to succeed. I value relationships as well as results, and work to embody my values in all decisions and actions.
>
> People can expect the following from me:
>
> - A listening ear to understand the dreams and desires of the people I work with
> - A clear picture of where we are going
> - A structure that provides for challenging yet achievable goals and objectives
> - Direction and involvement based on a person's level of knowledge and commitment to the task
> - An environment that fosters the following:
>   - The importance of worthwhile work
>   - Allows people to be in control of the goal
>   - Positive recognition

If you were to pull out three or four key concepts from Mark's leadership philosophy, you might highlight:

- Mark wants to be perceived as a humble servant leader.
- Mark inspires team members to perform well and continuously improve.
- Mark empowers people so they can succeed.
- Mark values people and relationships.

"Wait," you say. "What about clear communication, great listening skills, worthwhile work, and positive recognition?" Those are certainly valuable elements of Mark's leadership philosophy and of his daily interactions—but I selected the four elements that jumped out at me.

Hopefully I've got you thinking about what you might include in your leadership philosophy.

Let's get started. Consider these questions as you craft your personal leadership philosophy.

KEY ELEMENTS (PRESENT DAY)

What are your reasons for being a leader? Why are you serving in an influencing role today?

_____

_____

_____

_____

What results are your leadership efforts generating today? There might be positive and negative results—note them both.

_____

_____

_____

_____

Who am I serving today? Note the roles or (even better) the specific players you are leading.

_____

_____

_____

_____

What is the impact today of your leadership efforts on your relationships with the players noted in the preceding item? Note positive and negative impact.

_____

_____

_____

_____

DESIRABLE OUTCOMES (FUTURE STATE)

How might your personal purpose and values inform your effective leadership behaviors? For example, if a value you hold is "honesty," how might that be demonstrated when you are influencing effectively?

_____

_____

_____

_____

How might you effectively and kindly leverage current team member skills and competencies to deliver on promised performance?

_____

_____

_____

_____

How might you inspire future skill development in team members to deliver needed performance?

_____

_____

_____

_____

How will you gauge the quality of your relationships with team members? What indicators will help you understand that mutual trust and respect is present?

_____

_____

_____

_____

Let's pull from these elements to create an initial draft of your personal leadership philosophy.

What are your two to three foundational beliefs about leadership? How do these beliefs shape your daily plans, decisions, and actions when leading others?

_____

_____

_____

_____

How do your core values and behaviors "show up" when you're at your best and leading effectively?

_____

_____

_____

_____

What gets in the way of you leading from your best self, modeling your beliefs and values?

_____

_____

_____

_____

What can people you lead expect from you in day-to-day interactions? How will you ensure you're leading from your best self?

_____

_____

_____

_____

Your responses to these questions will form the foundation of your personal leadership philosophy. It won't be a simple, crisp, bumper sticker statement. It will likely be a few paragraphs in length to adequately describe some details of your leadership beliefs, values, hurdles, and expectations.

There will probably be elements in your leadership philosophy that are aspirational—you're working on them; you aren't "there" with those elements yet. That's good. Formalizing and sharing these desired behaviors helps you align daily practices to them.

Have discussions about your leadership philosophy with your direct reports. Invite feedback from them so you can understand the perspective of your "first customers," the people you're trying to inspire daily.

Review your philosophy statement at least annually to make needed refinements and tweaks.

Be as intentional about your leadership philosophy as you are with your personal purpose, values, and behaviors. Align to them, seek feedback on them, refine them, and align again.

Continue this process throughout all your days. You'll contribute to better relationships, better team performance, and greater workplace inspiration daily.

Live Well to Serve and Lead Well

How do you feel, right now, as you read this section?

Are you healthy—physically, mentally, and spiritually? Are you fully present, engaged, and maybe even optimistic about what's to come today and in the days ahead?

Or do you feel like you're fighting a losing battle, sleep-deprived, or without a clear head, heart, and spirit?

If you are feeling less than your best self, you are unable to serve others well or to lead others well.

Living healthy is the foundation of effective service and leadership. It must come first.

What is a desirable standard for physical well being? You don't have to be a triathlete to qualify as "living well." But you do need to know where you stand, assess your physical well being, then refine it if needed.

A commonly used metric for physical health is BMI[2] (body mass index), which uses height and weight to assess the percentage of your body fat. It's not the only metric you should use, but it's a fast and easy way to gauge how close you are to a healthy weight.

Another valuable metric for physical health is to assess how you *physically feel* on a regular basis. If you have positive physical well being, you feel energetic, optimistic, present, and enthused about life. Though your feelings about your physical health are a subjective measure, it is an important element of your well being.

There are two main contributors to your BMI and your physical well being: food and exercise.

Food is fuel. The human body is a machine that expends energy in daily activities. How you fuel your body contributes to your positive physical well being or to your less than positive physical well being.

Traveling for client work and a sincere love of food caused me to struggle with my weight for years. The first food/fuel system that has made sense to me is Tim Ferriss's Slow Carb[3] diet. The basics are to eat lean proteins and vegetables, and to eliminate dairy, starches, grains, and fruits.

Slow carb meals are simple and tasty. Once your body gets used to your slow carb fuels, you feel stronger, more present, and happier. Even better: The diet includes one day off a week, where you can eat anything you want! This cycling of high calories actually helps the body's metabolism.

The "no grains or flour" core of the slow carb diet is reinforced in Dr. David Perlmutter's 2013 book, *Grain Brain*.[4] Perlmutter's research shows that eating whole grains can cause dementia, ADHD, anxiety, chronic headaches, and depression.

Another key part of improving your physical well being—and feeling stronger and better—is to *eat breakfast*. According to a 2011 NPD Group study,[5] 31 million people in the United States skip breakfast. Numerous studies[6] link skipping breakfast to increased risk of diabetes and coronary disease, as well as a steady, eroding effect on mood, memory, and metabolism.

Try this proven slow carb approach. Start small: Commit to eating a slow carb breakfast every day for two weeks. Tim Ferriss gives tips on a three-minute slow carb breakfast[7] if you're time crunched in the mornings (like many of us).

See how the slow carb breakfast makes you feel in those two weeks. If the slow carb breakfast works for you, incorporate slow carb foods into the rest of your daily meals.

You don't have to count calories on this diet. I didn't for the first year (but I do now).

My experience with the slow carb diet has been very positive. I lost 20 pounds in the first six months on the diet.

My wife, Diane, was concerned about this "fad diet" I'd jumped into. She was pleased that I was losing weight and fat—but the diet was inconsistent with the "four basic food groups" she'd been raised on. For example, one no-no on the slow carb diet is fruits and juices, because of their high sugar content.

I promised Diane I'd go to the doctor, explain the diet to him, and get tests run to make sure I wasn't doing any long-term damage to my physical self. I appreciated her concern. I'm a heart patient (I had a myocardial infarction in December of 1993) so I do have to watch my blood chemistry closely.

Six months after starting the diet I had a full blood panel work up.

When I saw my doctor a week later, he was thrilled at my weight loss and said my "color" was better than ever (not sure exactly what that meant, but he was pleased). The blood panel was the best I'd ever had. Cholesterol was 89, triglycerides were 50, HDL (good blood lipids) was 42 (anything above 35 is good for this body), and LDL (bad lipids) was 48.

The other key blood panel metric we watch is the ratio of HDL to total cholesterol, which we want below 4.5. My ratio that day was 2.55—the lowest ratio I've ever experienced.

Clearly the slow carb diet works for me. As of this writing I'm 3.5 years on this approach. I've lost a total of 25 pounds and kept it off.

When I travel, I'm able to order foods that keep me on the diet—lean proteins, lots of vegetables, no starches.

I continue to lose body fat. I've had to buy new, smaller pants. I've had to have my watches and rings resized. I've had to cut two inches out of my belts. Trust me when I say it is very gratifying to make these changes!

I have more energy, I'm more present, and I feel better.

Adding exercise will help you feel better, stronger, sooner. The simplest exercise is walking. Walking takes no special gear or health club membership. It is a form of exercise readily accessible to all of us.

Recent studies[8] have found that as little as 10 minutes of walking a day improves cardiac heath and cognitive memory. Start slow and build up to 30 minute walks once a day.

To help increase your physical activity, consider getting an activity/step tracker to help you monitor your fitness goals. The Fitbit One is a device recently top rated by *Consumer Reports*.[9]

You may find that your physical well-being doesn't need attention. If it does, maybe some of these ideas can help you manage your BMI and activity levels.

The healthier you are, the better you'll be able to manage being a visible, proactive champion of your team or company's desired work environment.

SERVANT LEADERSHIP IS THE FOUNDATION

If I have inspired you to take steps (literally and figuratively) to boost your physical health, let's look at the foundation of leading others effectively: servant leadership.

Serving others is the foundation of citizenship in our families, workplaces, and communities. The call to service has been described for centuries. It is found in nearly every one of the world's religions.

I define servant leadership as a person's dedication to helping others be their best selves at home, work, and in their community.

Anyone can serve—and lead—from any position or role in a family, workplace, or community.

What is the philosophy of servant leadership? You must understand and embrace the philosophy before your daily plans, decisions, and actions can be consistently aligned to that philosophy.

Servant leaders believe:

- Every person has value and deserves civility, trust, and respect.
- People can accomplish much when inspired by a purpose beyond themselves.

It is the servant leader's role and responsibility to enable others to bring their best to every moment and every interaction, at work, in their communities, with friends, or with strangers.

What are the practices of servant leaders? Servant leaders typically:

- **Clarify and reinforce the need for service to others.** They educate others by their words and actions. They help create a clearer understanding of the greater purpose of serving others. They pose questions to help those around them consider how to set aside self-serving behaviors and embrace servant leadership behaviors.
- **Listen intently and observe closely.** They understand that, in order to inspire the best in others, they must understand the world others live in. They do not assume things about others,

nor do they judge others. Over time they learn about their players' unique worldview and opportunities to serve by listening more than talking, observing more than preaching.

- **Act as selfless mentors.** They are not looking for credit! They are looking to boost traction in others' efforts to better serve. Their interactions and communications are designed to boost others' servant philosophy and others' servant skills.

- **Demonstrate persistence.** They understand that a conversation or two may not change a player's mind-set or assumptions. Servant leaders are lovingly tenacious; they invest hours in conversations over months to help educate and, hopefully, inspire servant leadership practices in others.

- **Lovingly hold themselves and others accountable for their commitments.** Servant leaders are human; they'll make mistakes. They know the players they are working with will make mistakes. And, they push for high standards of performance, values alignment, and service quality by everyone. They praise aligned behaviors and redirect misaligned ones to create consistent service to others.

These practices are vitally important for leaders of culture-change efforts in their team or company. Your leadership philosophy reflects your beliefs and your desire to be of service to others. Your organizational constitution will outline how your team or company's work environment necessitates dignity, respect, and cooperation in daily interactions.

Helping your organization's leaders and employees align to these new rules of engagement requires that you be a *model* of servant leadership, a *coach* of servant leadership, and a *champion* of servant leadership.

How do you know if you are a servant leader? You don't have a vote! The only folks who *do* have a vote are those that interact with you daily: work colleagues, customers, friends, and family members. You must ask regularly, "How can I be of greater service to you?" then refine your behaviors to serve more effectively.

Your servant leadership approach will help leaders' and team members' contributions and engagement.

Team member *contributions* are the result of the application of every team member's knowledge and skills in service to the organization's goals. Team members deliver on performance promises daily.

Team member *engagement* comes from each person's feeling of trust and respect in the workplace, of values alignment by leaders and peers, and of doing meaningful work, every moment.

Your servant leadership and culture refinement efforts can result in consistent contribution from every team member as well as demonstrated engagement by each team member, *every day*.

Don't leave team member contributions and engagement to chance. Be intentional by clarifying and sharing your personal constitution, which includes:

- Your personal purpose, values, and valued behaviors
- Your leadership philosophy, based on the foundation of servant leadership

Then, live in alignment with your personal constitution, in and out of the workplace.

Let's transition to creating the elements of your organizational constitution. The next chapter helps you craft your organization's reason for being—its present day purpose.

CHAPTER 3

Clarify Your Organization's Purpose

C ompany mission or purpose statements have been around for many years. For example, Nature Publishing Group's first mission statement was formalized and published in 1869.[1] Mission or purpose statements came into vogue for many businesses in the 1960s and in the years since.

Research[2] indicates that mission or purpose statements are consistently beneficial to companies' success and long-term survival.

What is your team or company's raison d'être, its reason for being? Why does it exist? Whom does it serve? Why should customers—or even employees—care about your team or company?

I want you to do some research before you go any further in this chapter. Ask 10 people in your company or on your team what the purpose of your company or team is.

Take notes. You might even video them answering this question.

Unless your team or company has been intentional about its reason for being, it is likely that you will hear very tactical ideas about your team's purpose. Respondents will typically say things like:

- We print catalogs (or sell cars or make medicine or deliver whatever your core product or service is).

- Our purpose is to make money for stakeholders or stockholders.

When you pose this question, you might hear some exasperation in respondents' voices or see it in their body language. They may feel as if there is a different answer you're looking for and that they should know what the real answer is, or that the question is dumb because "everybody knows what we make here."

We should not be surprised by the responses to this key question. In the absence of clarity, with no formal declaration of purpose or mission, the practical reality of day-to-day activity becomes the accepted focus, the norm. "What we do" becomes employees' total understanding of the business.

"To make money" becomes the entire reason for the team or company's activities.

The problem with this practical view is that it is simply not inspiring for the majority of players in your organization. Nor is it particularly relevant to them in their daily roles.

Making catalogs is a very tactical activity. So is selling cars or selling sandwiches. We're never done. Tomorrow, there will be many more catalogs to print, more cars to sell, more sandwiches to make. *Activities* are never-ending.

Activities are not, by themselves, inspiring to us humans.

You and I both know that making money is a very good thing for organizations. If companies are profitable, they can hire more people. They can impact more lives. They can reach more customers. They can improve more communities, and so on.

However, if employees see making money as the *primary* purpose of your business, they're not going to be personally motivated by it.

Employees don't make big money. Shipping more catalogs today does not impact their paychecks or bank accounts tomorrow. Employees are not typically stockholders or owners of the company. Someone else makes more money when product goes out the door—not employees.

The company making money is someone else's reality. It is not inspiring to team members, from moment to moment.

Culture Effectiveness Assessment #3: Inspiring Purpose	Strongly Disagree	Disagree	Slightly Disagree	Slightly Agree	Agree	Strongly Agree
1. Clarity of Purpose Our team or company's purpose statement is succinct and specific.	1	2	3	4	5	6
2. Our Purpose Serves Customers Our purpose statement describes how we improve our customers' quality of life.	1	2	3	4	5	6
3. Our Purpose Is Well-Communicated Our published statement is known; team members can repeat it nearly verbatim. The statement is visible in communications and discussed in meetings regularly.	1	2	3	4	5	6
4. Our Purpose Serves as an Active Guidepost Our team's or company's strategies, goals, plans, decisions, and actions are examined through the lens of our purpose statement. If aligned, they're acted upon. If not, they're set aside.	1	2	3	4	5	6
5. Customers Understand and Believe Our Purpose Internal and external customers can explain our purpose statement and offer examples of how our purpose is demonstrated in our interactions with customers.	1	2	3	4	5	6

Let's look more closely at purpose statements.

I use the terms *mission statements* and *purpose statements* interchangeably. In my experience, these terms refer to what a business's reason for being is *today*, as opposed to a vision statement that is a description of the organization's desirable future state.

My experience and research lead me to believe strongly that the "present day" description is a stronger foundation for teams or companies embarking on the journey to high performance and values alignment.

A clear purpose statement is actionable, tangible, and relevant for members of your team or company.

What Is an Effective Purpose Statement?

A "present day" purpose statement, in its most perfect form, is an inspiring and compelling description of what your company or team tries to accomplish on a daily basis.

Your team or company's purpose statement needs be compelling and inspirational! It should clearly describe what you and your team members are passionate about.

Let's define an organizational purpose statement as a succinct declaration that explains what your company does, for whom, and to what end—why customers should care about what your company does and what it stands for.

Unfortunately, most organizations do not have a clearly defined purpose with these three elements. A few don't have a formal statement of mission or purpose at all.

Let's look at a few mission and purpose statements from real companies. I've grabbed these mission or purpose statements from the company websites (links are in the notes for your viewing pleasure).

We'll examine what elements these statements include and which ones they are missing:

Creating superior value for our customers, employees, partners and shareholders.[3]

Is it clear what the company does? No—there is no reference to the company's products or services (it is a tire company). The statement does reference "superior value," but doesn't define what that value is. Is it profits? Is it a good value purchase for a consumer? It could mean either or both of these values—but it is not clear.

Is it clear for whom the company does it? Yes—it aims to create superior value for its customers, employees, partners, and shareholders.

Is it clear to what end employees toil or why customers should care? No—there is no desired end state described beyond the hard-to-nail-down "superior value."

To nourish and delight everyone we serve.[4]

Is it clear what the company does? It aspires to nourish, which gives us a hint about its business (restaurants). I like this reference—and would like it better if it were a bit more descriptive.

Is it clear for whom the company does it? "Everyone we serve" is the target market. That can include customers, employees, and stakeholders. The broad reference is interesting—and I would appreciate more specificity.

Is it clear to what end employees toil or why customers should care? The company aspires to delight, not just nourish. I think, yes, it does cover this element nicely—and succinctly.

To discover, develop and deliver innovative medicines that help patients prevail over serious diseases.[5]

Is it clear what the company does? Yes—it discovers, develops, and delivers innovative medicines.

Is it clear for whom the company does it? Yes—it does it for patients who are battling serious diseases.

Is it clear to what end employees toil or why customers should care? Yes—they help those patients prevail to win those battles.

I think this is a very effective purpose statement.

To inspire and nurture the human spirit—one person, one cup and one neighborhood at a time.[6]

Is it clear what the company does? Yes—it aspires to inspire and nurture the human spirit. Exactly how it does that isn't clear, though (it is if you understand that this is Starbucks' purpose statement).

Is it clear for whom the company does it? It is not exactly clear whose human spirit will be inspired and nurtured. We might make the assumption that the company aims to inspire and nurture customers, employees, and neighborhood members—but it is not clearly stated.

Is it clear to what end employees toil or why customers should care? Yes—inspiration and nurturing are valuable outcomes to strive for, both for individuals and for neighborhoods.

This statement is 90 percent there! The assumption required of what is in the "one cup" makes the reader work a bit harder to understand what this company does.

I am confident that this purpose statement is crystal clear in the hearts and minds of Starbucks employees today. (We'll learn more from Starbucks' CEO, Howard Schultz, later in this chapter.)

> *To build a sustainable mining business that delivers top quartile shareholder returns while leading in safety, environmental stewardship and social responsibility.*[7]

Is it clear what the company does? Yes—it is a mining business.

Is it clear for whom the company does it? Yes—it does it for shareholders. Customers and employees are not referenced in this statement.

Is it clear to what end employees toil or why customers should care? The primary output is the benefit to investors, to the shareholders. Employees might be inspired by the emphasis on safety. Customers might be inspired by the aspiration of environmental stewardship and social responsibility. However, it is clear that this company sees its primary reason for being as making money.

Let's add one more statement to analyze—your company's mission or purpose statement. Fill in the blanks after each of the questions that follow.

My company's mission or purpose statement: (*Note:* Where will you find your team or company's purpose statement? If you can't find a formal statement, you will have a tough time completing these questions.)

_____

_____

_____

Answer these questions about the key elements that effective purpose statements include:

Is it clear what your company does? Why or why not?

_____

_____

_____

Is it clear for whom the company does it? Be specific.

_____

_____

_____

Is it clear to what end you and your peers toil or why your company's customers should care?

_____

_____

_____

With these examples—and your company's own—we can see that it's not easy to craft a purpose statement that addresses all three questions crisply, invitingly, and succinctly.

Remember that making money is not a differentiator for your organization. It is a requirement for survival for all companies, though. Profits are a good thing! And, as we've discussed, making money is a practical yet ultimately deflating reason for being. It does not inspire employees or customers.

Making money, as an outcome, doesn't need to be formalized in your team or company's purpose statement.

We'll guide you through creating or refining a more effective purpose statement for your team or company in a few pages.

COMMUNICATING YOUR COMPANY'S REASON FOR BEING

If your company has a mission or purpose statement, how well do employees know it and believe it?

Research published in 2008 by the Institute for Corporate Productivity indicates that while 84 percent of organizations studied have published a mission statement, 62 percent of those companies said that just *half of their employees could repeat the company mission statement* if asked.[8]

Although more than two-thirds of the 262 responding companies said that their mission statements had been effectively communicated, most employees in the surveyed companies don't know their organization's purpose statement well enough to repeat it.

This smells a lot like the logical consequences of "managing by announcements," a viruslike plague I call "MbA."

When infected by MbA, leaders do a good job of *defining* purpose or policies or procedures; they *publish* and *announce* the details, and then expect all employees to immediately *align* to them.

Leaders believe, "We've told them, so now they know, and now they'll do what we've told them."

How does a leader check that assumption? Ask and observe— often. It is likely you'll find that too few leaders or employees are able to repeat the purpose or policies or procedures to you.

Simply announcing new practices or policies or a purpose statement isn't enough.

Without reinforcement of the new practices, without context for why these changes are necessary, employees don't have any compelling reason to embrace or demonstrate the new purpose or policies or procedures.

To ensure that desired changes take hold—like employees knowing and believing in a revised purpose statement—leaders will need to invest time and energy to thoroughly and consistently *educate* players about the desired changes.

Then leaders must spend time and energy—roughly 10 times the time and energy spent developing the new practices—to ensure the desired changes are embraced. Leaders must model the changes, coach to the changes, praise progress as people embrace the changes, redirect players who aren't embracing the changes, and so on.

I'll outline specific steps for communicating and reinforcing your organizational constitution—including your purpose statement—in Chapter 5.

What Is Your Team or Company's Actual Purpose?

Sometimes the desired purpose statement is well written, thoroughly communicated, even posted throughout the organization, and so on—but *it isn't lived*.

In these situations, the *actual* purpose—the purpose demonstrated from day to day—is much different than the *desired* purpose of the company.

Here's a prime example. One company's mission statement:

To become the world's leading energy company—creating innovative and efficient energy solutions for growing economies and a better environment worldwide.

Let's go through the elements of an effective purpose statement.

Is it clear what this company does? Yes—it aspires to create innovative and efficient energy solutions.

Is it clear for whom the company does it? Yes—it serves growing economies (which is a pretty broad marketplace).

Is it clear to what end employees of the company toil or why customers should care? There seem to be two competing outcomes in this statement—being the world's leading energy company and creating a better environment worldwide.

Do you sense the underlying theme of this company's purpose statement? Its reason for being seems to be making money.

Which company is/was this?

Enron.

The company's *actual* purpose—as demonstrated by senior leaders—was discussed in a 2007 interview with Enron vice president Sherron Watkins. Watkins was one of many senior leaders at Enron who raised questions, concerns, and fears about the company's accounting practices with the CEO—to no avail.

In the interview, Watkins said the core problem at Enron was "greed and arrogance" among executives.

She explained, "Enron's leaders set the wrong tone. So did Arthur Andersen's leaders [Andersen was Enron's external auditor]. In the end, both companies put revenues and earnings above all else. The means by which those earnings were generated did not matter. Were laws broken? Yes. Were lives devastated by it? Yes."[9]

Enron is not alone. Accounting scandals have been the undoing of Waste Management (1998), WorldCom (2002), Tyco (2002), Health-South (2003), Freddie Mac (2003), American International Group (2005), Lehman Brothers (2008), Bernard Madoff Investment Securities (2008), and Satyam (2009).[10]

We could track down the purpose statements of any of these organizations and find that their mission or purpose statements did not specifically say, "Company executives shall lie, cheat, and steal our way to billions of dollars."

Yet that's exactly what happened in these companies.

The credibility of any team or company—and its senior leaders—is based on the team or company doing what it says it will do, living its defined purpose, and aligning to its defined values.

If the *actual* purpose being pursued is different than the *desired* purpose, the organization is living a lie—and eroding its credibility with employees, customers, and stakeholders.

HUMANS ARE DRAWN TO AND INSPIRED BY GREAT PURPOSE

In his best-selling book, *Drive*, Daniel Pink examined what motivates people. He said humans, "by their nature, seek purpose—a cause greater and more enduring than themselves."[11]

In a recent interview, Starbucks CEO Howard Schultz told Oprah Winfrey, "It's not what you do; it's *why you do it* that is important!"[12]

Schultz described the "spiritual crisis" that Starbucks created for itself in the beginning of the recent global recession. Despite record growth and profits, the company had stepped away from its core purpose and values.

Starbucks, Schultz says, was measuring and rewarding the wrong behaviors. Starbucks' purpose and values "were compromised by yields and profits," he said—and he took personal responsibility for that.

The turnaround began with an apology delivered in person by Schultz to more than 10,000 partners—store managers and employees. He asked these key players to help him and the company focus on "the only number that matters: one cup, one customer, one experience, one employee at a time."

Schultz realized that he and Starbucks' senior leaders had to regain the trust of store managers and employees first. If they could regain the trust of these key partners, they might have a chance to regain customers' trust over time.

In the five years following that epiphany, Starbucks regained that trust and has returned to being a company of which employees and customers are proud.

There is one other tangible benefit to having an effective purpose statement.

Your purpose statement serves as an *active filter* to assess opportunities, plans, decisions, and actions. Leaders and team members can easily pose the question, "Does this opportunity or action align with our defined purpose, our reason for being?" If so, it makes sense to pursue that opportunity, to take that action.

If not, it is easy to see—and to communicate—that it doesn't make sense to pursue that opportunity. In fact, pursuing a misaligned opportunity or action wastes time, money, and human energy.

Having a clear, effective purpose statement helps the company or team stay confidently on track.

CRAFTING A COMPELLING, INSPIRING PURPOSE STATEMENT

Before we get you started on creating or refining your own team or company purpose statement, let's take a moment to consider companies that you regard highly, that you enjoy experiencing.

It could be your local espresso bar, or your dry cleaners, or your dog groomer. One of my favorite local providers is a tiny hair salon. Doreen is happy, friendly, and extremely competent. She is very flexible, cutting my hair at odd hours at times, due to my travel schedule.

Your favorite providers may not have a formal purpose statement, but they have successfully and consistently wowed you as a customer, delivering more than you expect time and time again.

Consider how your favorite providers make you *feel*. If they make you feel important or valued or part of the family, how do they accomplish that?

What can you learn from how they make you feel valued, and bring that feeling into your team's or company's purpose statement? Feel free to make notes below. Be specific: How do your favorite providers make you feel important and valued? What do they *do* that makes you feel valued?

_____

_____

_____

Now let's look at an excellent example of a purpose statement from one of my culture clients:

> Our purpose is to deliver quality, on-time product marketing communications solutions that inspire consumers to purchase our customers' products and services.

This is a clear statement of *what the company does* (quality marketing communication solutions), *for whom* (its customers), *so that* consumers buy its customers' products and services.

This company's succinct, crisp purpose statement is compelling and inspiring for employees! The statement educates them about *why* what they do each day is important to their customers. More important, the clarity that comes from this purpose statement boosts employee pride and enthusiasm for their work each day.

Building this purpose statement took months of honest assessment and intense discussions among and between leaders, managers, team supervisors, and frontline team members.

When the senior leadership team took this statement (draft #40, give or take!) to organization members, employees smiled and nodded. They said, "Yes, that's exactly what we do!"

With those smiles, nods, and responses, the senior leadership team knew they had removed all the jargon and buzzwords. They had successfully crafted a statement that described the *core compelling essence* of their organization—its reason for being.

Here is another example from a very different "organization." I'm a working musician in my free time.[13] The band I've been performing with since 2006 is filled with amazingly talented, fun, funny, and values-aligned teammates. We've all been around the music industry for many years—most of us on the periphery, some very much in the thick of things.

The age range of our team (six performers and a full-time sound engineer) is 40 to 65 years of age. We're beyond the "we're going to make it big" or "we're going to make money" hopes of younger musicians getting started in the music business.

There are a lot of moving parts to our shows, just as in your companies and teams. Only when our team's players are aligned to a common purpose and shared values can the work (loading gear, driving long hours, setting up gear, sound checking, performing, tearing down, loading the trailer, driving long hours, etc.)—and the show—go smoothly.

The band's purpose statement is:

> With trusted friends, to present top-quality performances that wow and inspire audiences, create positive relationships, and generate return engagements.

Let's examine how this statement incorporates the elements of an effective purpose statement.

What do we do? We present top-quality performances with trusted friends.

For whom do we present these performances? We present to customers that hire us (more than once, we hope).

To what end do we toil? Why should customers care? We perform such that audiences are wowed and inspired. We engage our audiences so they're dancing and singing right along with us. They love our talent and our performance so much, they ask us back again.

Purpose statements are powerful drivers of clarity and inspiration in all kinds of organizations, even bands and families!

Let's get started on your purpose statement.

The next few steps will help you create a meaningful first draft of your company or team's purpose statement.

Before you start, let's prepare your body, mind, and spirit for this task. Take a deep breath—oxygen inspires your brain cells and heart muscles. Most of us take very short breaths—short in duration as well as in depth. Breathe deeply and slowly. It's okay—you won't pass out!

Stand and stretch your muscles for a minute or two—maybe shake out your arms and legs like an Olympic swimmer getting ready for a race. That'll get your blood flowing.

Sit comfortably—and relax. Most of us don't relax much at all during our daily activities—we hold our muscles tight, which inhibits effective blood flow and causes us to invest energy in tightness. Relax—loosen your muscles.

I encourage you to think beyond the first right answer that comes to mind. Note those right answers down—but know that the essence is more about the best answer than a right answer.

Dig deeper and look for what will both educate and truly inspire team members.

Let's begin:

1. List the **products or services** that your team or company delivers to customers day-to-day. What does your company make or deliver?

   _____

   _____

   _____

   _____

2. Who are your primary **customers**? Who seeks out your products and services? Whom do you primarily serve? List those individual players and/or teams or even companies you serve.

   _____

   _____

_____

_____

3. **To what end** are you and your team members toiling? What
    are the *benefits* that customers gain when they receive or use
    your products and services? How do your products or ser-
    vices improve their quality of life, boost efficiencies, or help
    move their organizations or communities or families toward
    desired goals?

    (These are harder questions to answer than the two first
    questions. These answers can move you from right answers—
    what our team makes—toward the best answers—*how our team
    inspires*.)

    _____

    _____

    _____

    _____

    Now, pull the most compelling, impactful answers from
    each of the three questions into a single purpose statement that
    clearly describes your team or company's reason for being.

    _____

    _____

    _____

    _____

Great work! You've got a solid draft of your team or company's
purpose statement.

Your work is only just beginning. Next you must socialize these
ideas—you must share this draft statement. Share it with peers, bosses,
and team members. You might even share it with key customers who
know your team or company well and can provide their insights.

Your stance during this sharing phase is not to justify or defend
terms or concepts in the purpose statement. Your stance is to learn

what others see in it, to engage others, and to understand their perceptions.

Listen to people's reactions. If the words in your draft statement don't ring true for 90 percent of your team's or company's members, you're not done with that statement yet.

You'll need to wordsmith it until it does ring true for the great majority of team members.

Ask team members for better words to describe your company's impact on customers. Words are powerful—the best words for your purpose statement will engage team members as well as customers. Keep searching for and testing better terms to describe your organization's beneficial impact on others.

Refine the statement and seek feedback again.

You may have to go through a few iterations to reach a purpose statement that you're satisfied with and that team members are drawn to and inspired by.

Nice job! Let's build on the foundation you've created with this purpose statement by adding standards for great team or company citizenship—values and valued behaviors.

CHAPTER 4

Define Values in Behavioral Terms

C ongratulations! You've finished your purpose statement, which outlines your team's or company's reason for being. You will soon begin the socialization of this draft purpose statement—and you will learn a great deal.

You will spend time and energy in refining the purpose statement. Every discussion, every dialogue, will bring greater clarity to you and your team members about your team's reason for being.

Now let's shift our focus to values.

The next step in creating your organizational constitution is to define the positive values and behaviors you want every leader and employee to demonstrate in every interaction with team members and customers.

Values—and values defined in behavioral terms—are the most important element of your organizational constitution. The values and behaviors that you decide are required in your team or company will be examined, judged, engaged with, and (it is hoped) embraced for years to come.

Values and valued behaviors are the most visible demonstration of your organizational constitution. Values and valued behaviors are the *evidence* of your constitution that is noticed by people—customers, potential employees, everyone who comes into contact with your team members.

Values and valued behaviors are the unique theme of your organization's culture that differentiates your company from other companies.

They attract like-minded (and values-aligned) potential employees and customers, and create heart-driven momentum that builds performance and engagement across the organization.

Two highly values-driven companies, Southwest Airlines and Zappos,[1] are examples of companies that hire and coach to their specific, defined, desired valued behaviors. With the right values, character, and heart in place, aligning skill sets to the role is easy.

Values alignment rarely happens casually. It happens so rarely that we can confidently say the chances of values alignment happening in your company or team *without intentional effort* are slim or none.

Culture Effectiveness Assessment #4: Values Expectations	Strongly Disagree	Disagree	Slightly Disagree	Slightly Agree	Agree	Strongly Agree
1. Clarity of Values Our team or company's values statement is formalized and publicized.	1	2	3	4	5	6
2. Our Values Are Measurable Our values are defined in specific, tangible, observable, and measurable behaviors.	1	2	3	4	5	6
3. Our Values Are Well-Communicated Our values, definitions, and behaviors are known; team members can repeat them nearly verbatim. Values expectations are frequently discussed in meetings (one-on-one, team, or total group meetings).	1	2	3	4	5	6
4. Everyone Is Held Accountable for Living Our Values Leaders and team members are expected to demonstrate our valued behaviors. Positive and negative consequences are promptly applied to ensure daily demonstration of our values and behaviors.	1	2	3	4	5	6

5. Customers Experience Our Values in Every Interaction	1	2	3	4	5	6
Internal and external customers see and hear our values being demonstrated at all times. If they don't know our values, they understand them after interacting with us over time.						

WHY DO YOU NEED VALUES DEFINED IN BEHAVIORAL TERMS?

Every company and team wants talented players that are *enthused* about their work and teammates, who are *willing* to learn and grow, and who *support* their peers through cooperative teamwork.

A positive attitude—by a leader or employee—is terrific to have in the work environment.

So, how does a leader ensure consistently great attitudes from the team's or company's players? Is the only way a leader can gain talented team members' enthusiasm, willingness, and support through attitude?

Can a leader *manage* a person's attitude? My research and experience leads me to believe that's not possible. By definition, attitude comes from *within* a person. Attitude is intrinsic, internal to each person—it isn't easily influenced by efforts from outside oneself.

A leader may try all kinds of ways to boost others' attitudes. However, I've not seen leaders be consistently successful at managing others' attitudes.

So, let's agree that leaders cannot manage a person's attitude.

Can you *hire* for attitude? I think many leaders would say they try to, but that it is very difficult to do. (We'll discuss hiring in Chapter 9.)

I've seen some very good leaders experience frustration when an employee's initially terrific attitude went downhill and nothing the leader tried could halt that attitude erosion.

NUTTERISMS

"YOU CAN'T MAKE UP IN TRAINING WHAT YOU LACK IN HIRING."

A team or company has the responsibility to hire team members with applicable skills, a willingness to learn and contribute, and aligned values and citizenship skills.

Once hired, potential stars require an extensive orientation and ongoing mentoring to find the best fit for their skills and passions.

If you don't hire for skills, willingness, and values, you're screwed.

So, we have to answer "no" to this second question.

Is attitude *measurable*? That is difficult to do, as well. Typically all we can do is observe people's behaviors—their plans, decisions, and actions—and attempt to *interpret their attitudes* from those plans, decisions, and actions over time.

Trying to measure attitude is more of a guess than a reliable assessment.

Let's agree that attitude is not consistently or reliably measurable.

So, can we agree that attitude is a difficult gauge of employee citizenship in your organization?

Separately, dare we agree that attitude is a difficult gauge of our *children's* citizenship in our families? That's a subject for another book—but it is also true; attitude is a difficult gauge of citizenship in nearly every circumstance.

Let's look at attitudes from another angle. You have served with talented, engaged team members in the past. They showed enthusiasm, willingness, and support of the team's work and of fellow team members. You might have said to yourself, "These people have great attitudes!"

Look deeper. Look at *how those players behaved*. Answer the question, "What did those team members *do* that made them such strong and aligned players?"

Did they:

- Consistently treat others with dignity and respect?

- Expect the best of others?

- Give others the benefit of the doubt?

- Accept responsibility?

- Never blame?

- Give credit?

- Praise and encourage?

- Express pride in the team's work?

You can probably add another three or four things—or a dozen things—to this list! Your great team members demonstrated their enthusiasm, willingness, and support through dozens of *observable behaviors* every day.

Their attitudes are reflected in these tangible, observable, measurable behaviors.

By looking at how great team members *acted* and what they *said*, you can define great citizenship behaviors that anyone can choose to demonstrate.

A key insight for you: You really don't have to care much at all about the attitudes of leaders and employees in your team or company. If they embrace the specific valued behaviors you define and they apply skills so team goals are met, that's all you need. That's all you can require of them.

Don't set yourself up to manage others' attitudes. What you need to do is *manage people's behavior*, which is much easier, more practical, and more effective to do.

YOUR BELIEFS MAY NOT BE ALIGNED

Just as managing others' attitudes is difficult or impossible, managing others' beliefs is equally difficult.

I am convinced that beliefs drive human behaviors. I believe that human beliefs, like attitudes, are intrinsic, internal to each person.

Unlike attitudes, though, I have seen behaviors change when people have been fully informed about what may be flawed beliefs. In a safe environment, people may be able to examine their beliefs and analyze whether those beliefs are causing them to behave in ways that are perceived as selfish, unethical, or worse.

Most of us humans do not examine our beliefs (or even our behaviors) from day to day—we just do things that seem to make sense to us.

I've seen flawed beliefs such as "I will do anything in my power to sell more widgets than my colleagues this year" drive behaviors like bending the rules, overpromising and underdelivering, lying and cheating, or cross-territory selling, to "sell more widgets."

I've seen flawed beliefs such as "She set me up to fail" drive behaviors like withholding key information, sharing partial truths, or "forgetting" to tell a colleague about a critical team meeting, to "get back at her for setting me up to fail."

If you're not seeing the behaviors you'd like to see in your workplace day to day, if colleagues do not demonstrate trust, dignity, and respect with each other or with customers, there could be flawed beliefs driving those behaviors.

And it is much easier, faster, and less complex to craft a workplace built upon desired, positive behaviors rather than try to change every player's unique beliefs.

BUILD YOUR VALUES FOUNDATION ON BEHAVIORS

To enjoy a values-aligned company or team, desired values must be intentionally defined in behavioral terms.

Once behaviorally defined, values must be modeled and measured to ensure alignment by all members of the organization in every interaction they engage in.

Most organizations, though, do not formally define their desired values. Only 33 percent of more than 400 global respondents of my Performance-Values Assessment[2] agree that their team has defined what a "good citizen" looks, acts, and sounds like.

The few companies that *do* define values unfortunately do little more than publish their values in some form (annual reports, posters in company facilities, possibly even printed on the backs of team member business cards).

Leaders in these organizations typically hope that, with the announcement or publication of the company values, people will automatically align to them. These leaders don't believe they have to do anything more. They are infected by the managing-by-announcements (MbA) plague.

This is all too common when looking at team or company values. Companies announce their values but *do not hold organization members accountable for demonstrating those desired values each day*.

There's a scientific term for values in that scenario; they're called *lies*.

The first lesson in this chapter is: "Don't publish values or behaviors if you're not willing to model, measure, and hold everyone in the company accountable for living those behaviors."

Though your company or team may not have formally defined values or behaviors in place today, your organization does have demonstrated values and behaviors. The ways people behave, interact, and operate have been reinforced over time. These ways are perfect; people are behaving exactly as we would expect them to behave, given the way the organization has guided and reinforced their behavior over time.

These ways of behaving become normalized (called norms). These ways are not formal, they're not explicitly communicated, and they may not be desired behaviors at all. But they have become embedded in your organization just the same.

Let me give you an example. One of my clients is a pharmaceutical company. Its campus is big, with office buildings, labs, manufacturing facilities, and the like spread across the property. The firm has grown so much that it has rented space in adjacent buildings. Shuttle buses run throughout the day to transport staff from one end of the expanded campus to the other for meetings and the like.

Years ago I found signs posted in every conference room on campus that made me laugh. Each sign said, "Meetings scheduled to start at the top of the hour shall begin no later than *ten minutes after* the top of the hour [italics mine]."

The signs—and this rule—gave everyone a 10-minute grace period for meetings scheduled to begin at the top of the hour (which nearly every meeting did). Guess what time meetings actually began? *Twenty minutes after the top of the hour!* The 10-minute grace period deserved a (you guessed it) 10-minute grace period.

I did some digging and learned that this 10-minute grace expectation began very early in the organization's history. In the manufacturing facility, quality checks happened at the top of the hour throughout two shifts. Since manufacturing staff had to complete these quality checks, the 10-minute grace period was granted so they could do their checks and scoot out to meetings by 10 minutes after the top of the hour.

Over time, the grace period rule gained strength. It was reinforced with the creation and posting of the signs. Despite the fact that the company had grown immensely since those early days—and that the great majority of meeting attendees were from functions other than manufacturing—the rule stuck.

Is that grace period rule serving the organization well today? Only the leaders of the organization can answer that question and modify the rule if needed. Have those leaders made that assessment? I can't tell you, as it has been a few years since I've been to this client's campus.

Here's another example. Another client had a very fancy executive dining room on-site, exclusively available to senior leaders of the organization. Starched white cloths covered each table. Heavy silverware and ironed linen napkins graced each place setting. Uniformed waitstaff moved quietly and efficiently to meet every need. Conversation was subdued, the tone professional.

Employees of the organization didn't enjoy quite such fancy accoutrements. The main cafeteria was loud and boisterous. The buffet featured hot and cold selections. The tables were plastic-topped, the eating utensils were black plastic, and the brown napkins were made of recycled paper.

When I questioned leaders and employees there, I heard no complaints or concerns about the executive dining room. No one could remember a time *without* the executive dining room; it had "always been there."

The undeniable issue is that the fancy executive dining room *separates leaders from employees*. It creates an "us and them" dynamic, a "haves and have-nots" dynamic that is difficult to justify, much less support.

The executive dining room raises questions for me about other benefits that might separate leaders from employees at this company. Is there separate executive parking? Are benefit plans different for executives than for employees? Are scholarship programs available to children of executives but not quite as available to children of employees? The list of questions goes on and on.

Leaders have to be careful. Policies and practices need to be fair and just for *all* players in the organization, not for a select few. Just because "we've always done it that way" doesn't mean practices shouldn't be evaluated for fairness and equity—and modified if needed.

STEP-BY-STEP GUIDELINES FOR CREATING VALUED BEHAVIORS

Since so few organizations—and so few leaders—have experience with defining valued behaviors for the organization, this next section is a how-to, step-by-step guide to creating them.

Leaders need to formalize three to five values with definitions and behaviors. Why three to five values? More than five are hard for us humans to remember and embrace! Don't complicate things by offering too much content; keep it simple and easy to remember.

As noted in the integrity value discussed in Chapter 1, the format for values statements looks like this:

Value: The one- or two-word value title.

Definition: A two- or three-sentence description that clearly states what this value means in your workplace.

Behaviors: These are "I" statements that explain exactly how you expect leaders and employees to demonstrate this value in your workplace. You will list no more than four behaviors per value. Why no more than four? Simplify, simplify, simplify.

Let's start with examples of well-defined valued behaviors from some of my culture clients.

Value: Service.

Definition: Our customers are the reason we're in business. By giving them superior service at every opportunity, we exceed their expectations. When we exceed their expectations, we're at our best.

Behaviors:

- I initiate friendly hospitality by promptly and enthusiastically smiling and acknowledging everyone who comes within 10 feet.

- I passionately exceed customers' expectations by offering solutions to their needs.

- I ensure that each customer is assisted in finding requested items.

- I deliver a clean, fast, friendly experience to every customer.

Is it clear what this retail client wants demonstrated regarding its customer service value? I hope you say, "Yes!"

The behaviors are where the values come to life. The behaviors are in "I" statement form—they state how every organizational member will behave when modeling this value.

The behaviors don't say, "I will . . . ." The term *will* is a future state. We don't want leaders or employees to *aspire* to doing this behavior—we want them to *do* the behavior. So, add no *will*s to your valued behaviors.

Here is example from another culture client:

Value: Mutual respect.

Definition: I work with my customers (internal and external) openly, honestly, sincerely, and ethically. I follow through on my commitments and expect the same from others.

Behaviors:

- I trust that everyone has the customers' and company's best interests in mind, so I attack problems and processes, not people.

- I don't take it personally when someone challenges a process I own. I listen to the input and implement changes to improve the process.

- I do not lie, betray a confidence, stretch the truth, or withhold information from a peer, customer, or stakeholder.

- If I am unable to keep a commitment or meet a deadline, I immediately inform all people who will be impacted.

Is it clear what this manufacturing client wants demonstrated regarding its mutual respect value? Again, I hope you can honestly say, "Yes!"

These particular "mutual respect" behaviors have struck a chord with a number of my culture clients. Many have used these behaviors in their own respect or trust values—so this good work has lived on and on.

One more example for you, this one from another culture client (a small family-owned business).

Value: Dedication and contribution.

Definition: Our company deserves our best. Each of us demonstrates dedication by applying our skills in service to company goals and customers, refining our skills to improve efficiency, boosting our own contributions, and valuing the contributions of others, daily.

Behaviors:

- I contribute my time, talent, and skills to the long-term viability of the company.
- I complete my tasks on time and under budget, fully responsible for the commitments I make.
- I embrace opportunities to build needed skills and increase my contributions as the business evolves.

Are these behaviors measurable? Can peers and customers provide feedback about the degree to which any leader or employee of this company is demonstrating these desired behaviors? I hope you agree with me that they are—and they can.

Your team or company's valued behaviors must outline observable, tangible, *measurable* actions. Just as organizational leaders manage to performance standards, these behaviors become values standards that are lived and proactively managed by leaders and employees throughout the company or team.

The Performance-Values Matrix discussed in Chapter 1 presents this idea in visual form. Leaders must set clear performance expectations and hold all accountable for those promises. And leaders must set clear values standards and hold all accountable for *those* promises.

High-performing, values-aligned teams and companies embrace the promises they make to each other and to customers. Those promises are based on performance expectations that must be delivered daily and on values expectations that must be demonstrated daily, by everyone— senior leaders, managers, team leaders, frontline experts, and everybody in between.

Your values and behaviors will outline exactly how your team or company's "great corporate citizens" look, act, and sound in your desired culture.

Let's get started!

First, consider values-aligned players already in place in your team or company today. It is very likely that you have benchmark, values- aligned players that you can learn from—and clone, over time.

Ask yourself, "How do our company or team great corporate citizens behave today?" What do they do today that makes you proud?

List these values or behaviors here:

_____

_____

_____

Add to this list any additional values you would like to see leaders and employees demonstrate with each other, peers, and customers. Consider the following values, which we also used in Chapter 2 to help you formalize your personal values.

Abundance	Freedom	Nobility	Service
Agility	Fun	Outrageousness	Significance
Audacity	Generosity	Passion	Stability
Brilliance	Harmony	Philanthropy	Teamwork
Creativity	Humility	Poise	Trust
Dream	Integrity	Proactivity	Valor
Excellence	Learning	Responsiveness	Wonder

Finally, think of providers you love to engage with—your favorite restaurant, hair salon, grocery store, gas station, and the like. What values do they espouse and demonstrate? List those, as well as one or two might be perfect for your team or company's values.

Now pull together your preferred values list. Identify three to five values you'd like every organizational member to model in daily interactions, and note them here.

_____

_____

_____

_____

Why three to five values? Why not 10? Remember, you're trying to create *clarity* about values and *alignment* to behaviors. Too long a list of values or behaviors causes confused inaction, not confident action.

We humans have limited working memories. Though we may attempt to do more in less time with multitasking, research shows that we don't perform well and don't retain information well if we're trying to do too much or learn too much at once.[3]

By limiting your values to three to five, you'll help create greater team member understanding, comprehension, and behavioral alignment of your desired team or company culture.

It is also much easier to communicate, educate, and reinforce a smaller list of values than a big list of values! This marketing effort for desired values and behaviors is an important part of implementing your organizational constitution, as we'll learn in Chapter 6.

DEFINE YOUR VALUES

Just as we helped you define your personal values, we must do the same for your team or company values. You must define your organization's values so that there is no question in anyone's mind about what exactly you mean by the value you want lived in your workplace.

In the absence of clear definitions, team leaders and members are left to figure out the definition on their own! You want shared values, however, so you can't leave your values definitions to chance.

Let's say one of your values is excellence. If you assume that, well, everyone knows what excellence means, you'll be unpleasantly surprised a lot of the time.

One player might define excellence as her personal best every day. Another might define excellence as hitting his goals by year-end (even if he is below goal at many points during the year). Another might define excellence as keeping the customer happy, while still another might define excellence as delivering the promised product or service before the deadline, at better than required quality, and at below the budgeted cost.

If each of these players aligns to his or her own definition of excellence, they'll all (1) be disappointed in their peers because they're not aligned with the same ideal, and (2) disappoint their peers because they're behaviors seem out of alignment!

This is a recipe for confusion, frustration, and conflict.

A clear, succinct values definition helps everyone know what each values standard is—and boosts confidence that everyone they work with holds the same values definition at the same time.

Define each value in *desirable* terms—say what it *is*, not what it isn't. You don't need to give examples; those we will cover with the specific valued behaviors for each defined value.

The definitions you map out in the following will be the foundation of the behaviors we'll define next, once the definitions are complete.

To further build your knowledge base of values and definitions, let's look at a few more examples from some of my culture clients.

Value: Excellence

Definition: I exceed the expectations of internal and external customers in every interaction.

Value: Respect

Definition: We treat everyone—team leaders and members, customers, and prospects—with the utmost dignity and honor. Every interaction leaves people feeling valued and trusted.

Value: Service

Definition: We engage internal and external customers with courtesy and the respect due to an honored guest. We exceed customer expectations every moment, confident they will enthusiastically share their experiences with others.

Value: Learning

Definition: We embrace the mind-set that there is always a better way. We learn from each other and from those outside our organization. We test new approaches to boost quality, efficiency, and stewardship of all resources.

Feel free to use these examples as templates for your team's or company's values definitions.

List your three to five values and add definitions for each value in the spaces.

Value: _____

Definition: _____

_____

_____

Value: _____

Definition: _____

_____

_____

Value: _____

Definition: _____

_____

_____

Value: _____

Definition: _____

_____

_____

Value: _____

Definition: _____

_____

_____

Include Observable, Tangible, and Measurable Behaviors for Each Value

The final and most important step in crafting your team or company values is adding behaviors to each value. Just as we defined your personal values in behavioral terms, we must do the same for your team or company's values.

I call these "valued behaviors" to differentiate them from any other behavioral guidelines that might exist in your organization. These valued behaviors build on the values definitions and describe exactly how you want members of your team or company to interact.

These behaviors define the playing field for great citizenship.

Here are a few more examples from clients to build up your valued behaviors knowledge base.

Value: Respect

Behaviors:

- I actively cheer others on by giving sincere praise and encouraging positive behaviors.
- I take personal responsibility to understand, respect, and appreciate others who are different from myself.
- I give honest and direct feedback by communicating in a respectful and timely manner.
- I respect customers and peers by using appropriate language at all times.

Value: Excellence

Behaviors:

- I embrace constructive feedback by taking personal ownership and changing my behavior to improve my contributions.
- I teach, train, and support the development of others by sharing my knowledge.

- I adapt to changing priorities by keeping myself informed about the business.
- I represent the company with pride by always following the dress code.

Value: Great place to work

Behaviors:

- I take responsibility for my actions, results, and mistakes.
- I consistently model high standards of performance, honesty, and integrity.
- I promptly and genuinely thank my fellow team members for both their efforts and their accomplishments.
- I demonstrate effective team membership, collaborating on plans and decisions, and delivering on my commitments.

Value: Safety

Behaviors:

- I follow all safety rules to the letter.
- I reinforce positive safety behaviors with others and challenge unsafe behaviors.
- I change my unsafe behaviors.
- I relentlessly create and sustain a clean, orderly work environment and work processes.

We'll start identifying your valued behaviors by brainstorming potential behaviors for each value. In the spaces that follow, note behaviors that you'd be proud to see team leaders and members demonstrate when they're modeling this value.

I use the term *demonstrate* intentionally. As noted earlier, you cannot measure or hold people accountable for what they think, what their attitude is, or what they believe. You can, however, measure and hold players accountable for demonstrating—acting on—clearly defined valued behaviors.

Note down potential fabulous team member (and team leader) behaviors for each of your values.

Value:_____

Definition: _____

_____

_____

Value:_____

Definition: _____

_____

_____

Value:_____

Definition: _____

_____

_____

Value:_____

Definition: _____

_____

_____

Next, cull through the behaviors you've noted to reduce the list to three or four behaviors per value. Really, identify at least three but no more than four valued behaviors; simplify, simplify, simplify.

These questions may help with your selection process. For behaviors you're considering, ask yourself:

- **Is this an observable behavior?** Can I assess someone's demonstration of this behavior by watching and/or listening to the person's interactions with customers, peers, or stakeholders? If not, toss it or refine it.

- **Is this behavior measurable?** Can I reliably score this behavior based on my observations of a player with others? Can I rank the degree to which a player models or demonstrates this behavior on a scale of low to moderate to high at any point in time? If not, toss it or refine it.

- **Is this behavior unique to a particular function or unit?** The behaviors for team or company-wide values must be global and relevant to all team members, no matter their role in the organization or function. If the behavior isn't one that is applicable and appropriate for any and all team members, toss it or refine it.

YOUR VALUES, DEFINITIONS, AND BEHAVIORS

Now, pull these important elements together. This pivotal piece of your organizational constitution adds depth and substance to the "values match" axis of the performance-values matrix discussed earlier.

This piece outlines what great corporate citizens in your team or company look, act, and sound like, every day.

Rewrite your values and definitions first. The rewriting will cause you to do some slight wordsmithing that will clarify the meaning of your values—to everyone's benefit!

The rewriting takes a little extra time, but it will help build clarity in your own mind, which is critically important.

Then, add your three or four valued behaviors, ensuring they outline tangible, observable, measurable behaviors for each value.

Value: _____

Definition: _____

_____

_____

Behaviors:

-   _____

- _____
- _____
- _____

Value: _____

Definition: _____
_____
_____

Behaviors:

- _____
- _____
- _____
- _____

Value: _____

Definition: _____
_____
_____

Behaviors:

- _____
- _____
- _____
- _____

Value: _____

Definition: _____
_____
_____

Behaviors:

- _____
- _____

- _____
- _____

Value: _____

Definition: _____

_____

_____

Behaviors:

- _____
- _____
- _____
- _____

Great job! You've got a solid draft of your team or company's values, definitions, and valued behaviors.

As with your purpose statement draft, your efforts with your drafted values, definitions, and behaviors are just beginning. Next you must socialize these ideas, sharing them with peers—other leaders and supervisors—and team members. You might even share them with key customers who know your team or company well and can provide their insights.

Just as before, your stance during this sharing phase is not to justify or defend terms or concepts in the values, definitions, or valued behaviors. Your stance is to learn what others see in the drafted values ideas, to engage others, and to understand their perceptions.

Ask for people's suggestions for better terms to describe what great team members ought to do and say in every interaction.

It's likely you've done a very good job with this draft, and not many suggestions or new terms will be offered. Keep the door open. Pose questions about different terms or behaviors. Ask, "Does this list fully define what our best team citizens do day in and day out? What are we missing?"

Listen to people's reactions. Again, if the words in your draft statement don't ring true for 90 percent of your team or company's members, you're not done with your values, definitions, and behaviors quite yet. You'll need to wordsmith it until it does ring true for the great majority of team members.

You may have to go through a few iterations to reach a values, definitions, and behaviors piece that you're satisfied with and that team members are drawn to and inspired by.

Before we leave this important element, let me remind you again about the danger of MbA—managing by announcements.

Defining your values and engaging team members in refining the definitions and behaviors will not, by itself, make yours a high-performing, values-aligned workplace.

Announcing values, definitions, and behaviors but not holding everyone accountable will erode the trust and integrity of your team, company, and leaders.

Let's look at another example of the negative impact of the plague of MbA.

A global organization was founded in 1869 and became a public company in 1999. In 2010 it reported net revenues of over $39 billion while employing more than 35,000 people. The company's business values[4] and principles were formalized in 1980. They include statements and definitions such as:

- Our clients' interests always come first.

- Integrity and honesty are at the heart of our business.

- We take great pride in the professional quality of our work.

- To breach a confidence or to use confidential information improperly or carelessly would be unthinkable.

The organization's list of values is extensive. All 14 of its values and business principles are desirable and honorable.

The problem? Leaders of this organization believed that the *publication* of their values and business principles *would ensure alignment* to them (a classic MbA symptom).

The result? In July 2010 the Securities and Exchange Commission (SEC) announced[5] that this organization, Goldman Sachs, agreed to pay a record $550 million fine to settle charges that the company misled investors in a subprime mortgage product just as the U.S. housing market began to collapse.

Since that time, Goldman Sachs has been attempting to reform its business practices through a new business standards committee, emphasizing individual and collective accountability. Time will tell whether these efforts will actually align behavior to the firm's desired values.

That's a hard lesson about the negative impact of MbA. There are many other examples we can reference but we won't take the time to do so here.

The good news is we can immunize you against the plague of MbA! That'll happen in Chapter 6, where we'll immerse you in the best practices of implementing your organizational constitution and managing to it, day in and day out.

Next we'll build on the terrific foundation you've created with your organization's purpose, values, definitions, and valued behaviors by adding standards for great performance in the form of strategies and goals.

CHAPTER 5

Outline Strategies and Goals for the Coming Fiscal Year

Τhis chapter explains what well-defined corporate strategies and goals look like. Leaders must clarify and consistently communicate strategies and goals, and then manage alignment of goals with strategies, values, and purpose.

Alignment ensures that talented, engaged team members know the right things to do and the right way to do them, and consistently deliver on them.

Your strategic plan is a formal statement of your company's desired path to success: what your customers want, what markets to pursue, what products or services to create, and how to deliver them profitably. Effective strategic planning and execution are built on cooperation among your organization's business units and support functions, sharing insights, opportunities, and even mistakes along the way.

Strategy is where the company's *vision of the future* intersects with the *realities of the now*, where traction is gained one product test and one happy customer at a time. Strategy provides a foundation for company goals, which outline the specific performance expectations for every team member, to ensure that the company stays on its desired path.

High-performing, values-aligned teams and companies are very intentional about strategic planning and goal setting. Goals cascade from company-wide targets (like "generate 10 percent market share growth in the next 12 months") to division targets (where R&D sets goals for new product releases and the marketing department outlines

NUTTERISMS

"YOU CAN SHOOT THE ARROW, THEN RUN OVER TO WHERE IT HIT AND DRAW A TARGET AROUND IT AND SHOUT 'BULL'S-EYE!' OR YOU CAN DRAW THE TARGET, SHOOT THE ARROW, ANALYZE THE RESULT, AND CLOSE THE GAP."

Be intentional with strategy and goals. Set the targets and let team members make their best efforts to contribute. Assess results frequently, refine efforts, and apply skills again.

Great team members know the target and refine efforts to keep those performance promises.

advertising and sales support, etc.), to department or team targets, and to individual player goal expectations.

Before we engage in our process for strategic planning and goal setting, I want you to take a moment and think about your most recent New Year's resolutions.

We humans are typically inspired each January to set personal goals for the coming year. We hope to increase our quality of life and build beneficial habits while quashing lousy habits.

Research by the University of Scranton[1] indicates that 45 percent of Americans usually make New Year's resolutions. The study found that the top five New Year's resolutions for 2014 are:

1. Lose weight.

2. Get organized.

3. Spend less, save more.

4. Enjoy life to the fullest.

5. Stay fit and healthy.

The problem with our New Year's resolutions is that we are really bad at honoring them! The same study found that only 8 percent of people are successful in achieving their resolutions. 49 percent have infrequent success, and 24 percent fail miserably on their resolutions each year.

Why do we humans struggle so much with our New Year's resolutions?

We may set the target unrealistically high. We may start out strong ("I'm going to run two miles after work four days a week!") but find that our bodies can't tolerate running or jogging that far or that often. By the end of the third evening's run, you've got muscle soreness that you never imagined! It hurts—so, you quit.

Another reason why we fail to keep our New Year's resolutions? We don't make our goals explicitly clear. This study found that people who explicitly make their resolutions are *10 times more likely to achieve their goals* than people who do not explicitly make resolutions.

One final contributor to our failure to keep our resolutions: We don't publish or share them with others in our world. Sharing our resolutions with others makes our goals *real* and *actionable*. Friends and family members can serve as cheerleaders when we make progress and as coaches when we fall short of our desired progress. They can even participate in our good habit building—eating healthier with us, power-walking with us, and so on.

To serve the technology-gadget lovers, there's a huge number of goal-setting apps[2] for our smartphones and tablets. These tools help track progress on your habits and goals, build a community of people who can support you (and whom you can support), and help your personal motivation with the very effective "streaks" method. You receive positive messages from the app when you put together "streaks" of beneficial habits. It could be 10 days of eating healthy foods, or six days of doing 30 minutes of brisk walking. Streaks help build desired practices into embedded habits.

What can we learn from people's best practices with their New Year's resolutions? There are many parallels between people accomplishing their personal goals and organizations accomplishing their business goals.

In my research and experience, I find that many teams and companies struggle to meet their performance commitments. Organizations that consistently exceed performance expectations rarely seek out an executive consultant like me!

The reasons why teams and companies don't perform to their potential are very similar to the reasons why we humans struggle to keep our New Year's resolutions:

- Targets are set too high.

- People do not have the skills required to meet performance standards.

- People are unable to sustain the new behaviors required to meet performance standards.

- Goals are not explicitly defined; they are not specific, measurable, or trackable.

- Goals are not shared with key players who can help celebrate progress, coach to realign, and so on.

Business goals represent a formal promise that's being made to customers—internal and/or external customers.

If goals are not met, then commitments are not met. When commitments are not met, your integrity takes a hit. Not only does your integrity take a hit, but the team, department, division, and so on experiences a hit to their integrity.

When integrity is eroded, customers can't trust future promises you make.

Mistrust builds on mistrust. And the cycle goes on and on.

It's an unhealthy cycle that costs you and your team trust, time, and money.

The antidote to these performance issues is a formal strategic plan that is aligned with your team or company's purpose, values, and behaviors. Your strategic plan will set forth specific performance goals that are required to gain traction on your desired strategic thrusts.

With your organization's purpose, values, and behaviors formalized, it's time to focus on your business strategic plan and performance goals.

What is your team or company's strategy? Don't go look it up. Just note here what you believe are your team or company's top three strategic thrusts right now:

1. _____

2. _____

3. _____

If you are like most organizations on the planet, describing your team or company's primary strategy or strategies isn't easy. For most companies, business strategy is not very clear. It isn't published. It isn't well communicated or well known.

Every organization needs to be intentional about its business strategy. With a formalized strategic plan, the right path is crystal clear. Goals are aligned to the strategy, and everyone understands why certain goals are a priority and other possible goals are not a priority.

Your business strategic plan becomes a filter for opportunities that pop up. Potential programs or products or services can be quickly assessed as to the degree to which they align with your business strategy. If they advance the strategy, they deserve further consideration. If they don't, they don't deserve time, talent, or funding.

Without a formalized business strategy, any path—any number of plans, decisions, and actions—can *seem* aligned to leaders and team members. People will make competing decisions that are misaligned with each other and with the overall strategy, which results in frustration (at minimum), chaos (at worst), inconsistent performance, and lousy customer experiences.

Other than that, everything is great!

A formal strategic plan helps everyone on the team (or in the division or company) understand what the business objectives are for the planning period and what goals and performance targets align with the business objectives.

How long should your performance period be? I recommend two years. In this shrinking global marketplace, a time frame longer than two years just doesn't offer many benefits. And a longer time frame can cause your strategic plan to be antiquated and off base. Little good can come of that.

A formal strategic plan outlines how the resources of the team or company will be allocated and aligned to deliver promised goals.

It answers the question "Why are we doing this goal, project, or task now?" *at any point in time* in the performance period.

It helps every leader and team member to be on the same page regarding your business strategy. It even helps every leader and team member communicate your strategy, in lay terms, to anyone they work with.

A formalized strategic plan removes any mystery. It creates clarity and confidence.

Once your strategic plan is formalized, you'll outline performance goals that align to the key elements of your strategy. Those goals will describe your desired metrics and targets, which, when met, ensure your strategy is being realized.

Some of you are thinking, "Strategic plans are different from business purpose and values, right? Strategies evolve constantly!" You're exactly right.

Jim Collins, the author of *Built to Last* and *Good by Choice*, described the shelf life of these key elements succinctly.[3] His research and experience lead him to suggest that, once clarified and validated, a team or company's purpose statement rarely changes. The same is true for your team or company's values—they rarely change.

Valued behaviors need to be refined over time. They will likely evolve as the team or company's culture evolves. Behavioral guidelines in the early stages of your organizational constitution may serve for a year or two, but require tweaks or additions to define your evolving team citizenship requirements.

Strategies evolve regularly. Strategies need close observation to ensure they're still relevant as your market changes, as your industry evolves, and as customer requirements shift. Make a formal reassessment of your team or company strategies every other year, more frequently if your strategies aren't serving your customers, your stakeholders, and your employees very effectively.

Goals change often. They are the tactical, day-to-day targets that ensure traction toward the accomplishment of your stated strategies. Projects come and go as aligned efforts deliver promised products and services.

You'll cycle in new goals and performance targets as your team or company learns and evolves. Some goals and projects might be found to be irrelevant or unneeded—despite how aligned they looked at the beginning of the performance period!

You've already built a strong foundation with your team's purpose, values, and valued behaviors. Now we'll build the framework for consistent performance with a strategic plan and specific goals.

This chapter's Culture Effectiveness Assessment allows you to rate how well your team or company's strategic plan and goals enable consistent performance.

Culture Effectiveness Assessment #5: Strategies and Goals	Strongly Disagree	Disagree	Slightly Disagree	Slightly Agree	Agree	Strongly Agree
1. Strategic Planning Our team or company engages in a disciplined strategic planning process at least every two years.	1	2	3	4	5	6
2. Specific Goals Our strategic plan includes specific, measurable, and time-bound goals that set desired targets for strategic imperatives.	1	2	3	4	5	6
3. Communication of Strategies and Goals Leaders and team members understand our strategic imperatives and goals. They can describe them in simple language quickly.	1	2	3	4	5	6
4. Reinforcement of Strategies and Goals Team members understand how their day-to-day	1	2	3	4	5	6

Culture Effectiveness Assessment #5: Strategies and Goals	Strongly Disagree	Disagree	Slightly Disagree	Slightly Agree	Agree	Strongly Agree
projects, goals, and tasks align to the strategic plan. Misaligned plans, decisions, and actions are redirected appropriately.						
5. Evolution of Strategies and Goals Goal traction is reviewed monthly. Goal refinement and adding new goals are common. Strategies are refined as needed during the performance period.	1	2	3	4	5	6

FIVE-POINT STRATEGIC PLANNING WHEEL

The great news about the organizational constitution work you've done so far is that you've already defined *who you are* as a team or company. Your purpose, values, and valued behaviors describe your reason for being, the principles that guide every effort, and the behaviors that you demand of great team citizens.

The five-point strategic planning process I recommend doesn't need to address the "Who are you?" question. It simply builds upon that foundation to ensure your team or company understands the pathway to performance success.

Once the pathway to performance success is clear, leaders can align team members' plans, decisions, and actions to exceed those metrics and targets.

Let's look at the five-point strategic planning wheel, depicted in Figure 5.1. We start this ongoing process at the upper-left of our graphic.

1. *Where*

> Where are we now? This first point enables leaders to take a close, honest look at what's working well regarding organizational performance. How are we viewed in our markets? Are our products or services unique and providing high value to

Figure 5.1   Strategic Planning Wheel

customers, or are our products and services seen as commodities? Or do we offer a mix across the value spectrum? If so, is that mix beneficial for our business and our customers today?

2. *What*

This second point focuses on future desirability and possibility. What opportunities or imperatives shall we consider? What are our customers looking for that might be in our team or company's "wheelhouse" (i.e., we do it well or have skills that can be realigned to do it well)? What opportunities will require us to conduct a skunk works, where we build or hire needed skills to pursue a desirable market opening?

3. *Decide*

Now you come to your decision point. This step typically requires the most focus and resolve. This is where you'll leverage your team or company's sweet spot, the combination of skills, vision, and ingenuity.

In point three you'll *decide* what three or four strategic imperatives your team or company will pursue over the next two-year performance period. Remember, keep it simple—no more than four strategic imperatives in your plan; three would be better! Once you've decided on your strategic imperatives, you'll *design* your plan to leverage strengths and test new pilot avenues. The design piece includes defining two or three specific goals for each strategic thrust. Design may also include reallocation of talent or funds, restructuring of your team or department, and so on.

4. *Work*

This point is where you'll spend the most time: working your plan. You'll put into place the elements you decided upon and designed in point three. You'll probably need to craft relevant performance dashboards that help communicate progress on strategies and goals with a quick glance. (There is a real art to creating relevant dashboards.) You'll need to communicate, educate, and promote your strategies and goals. You'll then align plans, decisions, and actions daily.

5. *Assess*

Point five is where you assess the progress on and effectiveness of your strategies and goals. This needs to happen often (quarterly works well). Gather data with key players, and, together, refine targets as needed. This assessment point enables you to evaluate your strategic imperatives for relevance at least every other year.

Effective assessment in point five serves as a lead-in to the next performance cycle's strategic planning—you'll go back to point one, and evaluate where the team or company is at, in terms of performing to plan. The cycle begins anew.

These five points are fairly typical of other strategic planning processes you may have used or experienced in the past. The terminology may be slightly different, but the flow from honest analysis to brainstorming, to deciding, to working, and to evaluation is a common step-by-step approach for strategic planning.

What is uncommon about our five-point wheel process is that it creates discipline. It creates clarity about strategies and goals. It clears and lights the path so that team members can apply their discretionary energy and skills toward the accomplishment of your team or company's strategies and goals.

This process will help your team or company keep its performance promises to customers and stakeholders.

Our five-point wheel process will help you plan and act intentionally, so you and your teams can not only *make* your performance resolutions but can *keep them*, every time.

Another uncommon piece of this process is that it *does not rely on a small group of executives* to craft a strategic plan independently, with little involvement by the team members who must put the plan into action.

Effective strategic planning, as outlined in the wheel, is a process of engagement and involvement by key players throughout the organization—executives, team leaders, and team members.

It involves *everyone*. Their involvement not only creates a clearer understanding of the strategic imperatives and goals, but it boosts buy-in and alignment of effort to those imperatives and goals.

Who Is in Charge of Communicating Your Business Strategies and Goals?

Years ago I observed a high-performing, values-aligned team engage in strategic planning, in the moment, right before my eyes.

This was in my YMCA executive days. I took a group of Los Angeles–area teenagers along with adult staff on a weeklong river rafting trip in Northern California.

None of the group members were experienced rafters. The rafting company staff spent a good three hours with us, teaching us paddling skills and teaming skills. That prepared us for our first day on relatively calm rapids—Class I and Class II.

As the week progressed, our skills grew and our experience helped us work better as a raft team.

Before taking us out on heavier rapids—Class III and III+—the guides would pull us out of the water on a beach. Then they would climb up a trail overlooking the rapids and scout out the safest passage.

These were dam-controlled rivers, so the degree of difficulty could change in an hour's time. The classification of the rapids could vary widely. Scouting three hours in advance might lead a guide to believe a particular route was safe—when it was not.

They watched the river flow, noting the safest passage. They then discussed and agreed on that passage. They mapped out which rafts would go first, second, third, and so on. Once the strategy was discussed and agreed upon, the guides trekked back to the beach. They explained what they had learned, and outlined the passage we would take.

We jumped in our rafts and "worked the plan." We listened to our river experts and rafted like pros, simply because we aligned to the plan that got us safely to the end of each run.

Our guides didn't scout Class II routes. Those had very clear channels for our rafts. Class III and III+ rapids were scouted *every time*.

Just as with the rafting company guides, every leader and team member is responsible for strategic clarity. Each team—leader/guide and members/paddlers—must understand the best passage to ensure safety and success.

Everyone needs to understand the strategic plan of his or her team. Team members must also know how that plan drives their functional contributions, their personal contributions to your strategic plan and goals.

Every team member should be able to describe how his or her daily projects, goals, and tasks contribute to the accomplishment of team or company strategies.

Specific, measurable targets help every player understand what performance is expected at what quality standard by when (what day or what time). Defined targets also help leaders praise aligned actions and redirect misaligned actions promptly.

Clarity of strategy and goals helps leaders and team members align plans, decisions, and actions that sustain the organization's performance over time.

The only way to ensure that everyone understands and can verbalize your strategic plan and goals is to communicate them effectively and to reinforce them regularly.

Every project team should be able to explain how their project contributes to one of the company's strategic imperatives.

Your performance planning process should link every performance expectation (be it a project, goal, or task) to a specific strategic imperative.

If it is difficult to describe how a project or goal does contribute to any of your strategic thrusts, it might be time to consider setting that project or goal aside.

The discipline required to align projects and goals to your strategic plan means that you'll periodically find that some projects or goals are misaligned. They simply fall outside your defined sweet spot, and have to be turned down.

MEASURE THE RIGHT THINGS

I spoke earlier about the art of crafting relevant performance dashboards.

Do you have performance dashboards readily available today to team members? Effective dashboards let team members see at a glance where they or their team stand in relation to standards at this point in time.

I've seen a variety of dashboards in place in client work environments. Some are computerized dashboards on big flat screen monitors. Some are traffic-light style, with performance that exceeds expectations in green, those just below standard in yellow, and those significantly below standard in red.

Some are sticky notes on a wallboard. So long as the performance data is current and relevant, that's what matters.

The problem is that sometimes the things that are easy to measure aren't the relevant things to measure. If you grab data from easy but irrelevant areas, you're not helping aligned performance—you're *eroding* it!

For example, the catalog printing group I worked with for many years had very large, very expensive digital printing machines. The built-in computerized dashboards could show how many impressions in how many minutes in a heartbeat.

The problem was that data on impressions per minute weren't the only relevant performance data they needed. If the job being run required John Deere green and the color was off a shade or two, the onboard dashboard might not catch that soon enough.

What do you call John Deere catalogs with the wrong green on the cover? Trash. You can't send them out; the customer—rightfully— demands its brand's proper green color.

So, the human operators needed to be observant and responsive. If the green color shifted, the operator had to stop the run, fix the color balance, and start the run again.

Stopping a machine running thousands of impressions a minute is expensive, but running the wrong color catalog is more expensive.

The operators had to learn the limits of the printing machine's cool built-in dashboard.

Here's another example. One of my clients ran a call center for loan customers. The computer software the firm used monitored each call—and the time duration of each call—very accurately. The dashboard showed who was running "long" on six calls during their shift. Great, right?

Not great. The desired time limit for calls was somewhat arbitrary; it was an average time frame target across each operator's shift. Some issues that customers had couldn't be addressed in the two-minute time limit, but operators were "dinged" for staying on one call too long.

When those operators pushed back, management realized that the software wouldn't be able to be the sole dashboard for operator performance each shift.

So, be aware of what you're measuring. If it's not relevant—or if it's only somewhat relevant—continue to refine your dashboard systems to improve their ability to measure the right stuff.

Build a Draft of Your Team or Company's Strategic Plan and Goals

The following steps will help you draft your thoughts on the five points of my strategic planning wheel.

Your responses will help you clarify the key parts of your desired strategies and goals—but they won't be the final strategic plan. As noted earlier, to ensure the best possible plan and goals, you'll welcome other key players into the discussion and the process. Their engagement and involvement will help refine the plan and goals—and will help build needed buy-in for the plan and goals!

First Point: Where

Where are we now? This first point enables you to take a close, honest look at what's working well with your team or company's performance. Are your team's products or services unique and do they provide high value to customers, or are your team's products and services seen as commodities? Where do you struggle to consistently exceed customer requirements?

Strengths: _____

_____

_____

Weaknesses: _____

_____

_____

Opportunities: _____

_____

_____

Second Point: What

What can you be? What opportunities or imperatives will you consider? What are your customers looking for that might be (or could be quickly) in your team or company's sweet spot? How might you leverage team skills and ingenuity profitably? What opportunities might help our company grow and succeed in new markets?

Imperatives: _____

_____

_____

Leverage strengths: _____

_____

_____

Opportunities: _____

_____

_____

Third Point: Decide

Now you come to your decision point. How will you leverage your team or company's sweet spot, the combination of skills, vision, and ingenuity?

What three or four strategic imperatives represent the best opportunities for your team or company over the next two-year performance period? Once you've decided on your strategic imperatives, *design* how to leverage strengths and test new pilot avenues. The design piece includes defining two or three specific goals for each strategic thrust. Design may also include reallocation of talent or funds, restructuring of your team or department, and so on.

Best opportunities to pursue:

1. _____

2. _____

3. _____

4. _____

Design: How will you refine the team's approach or structure for success?

- _____

- _____

- _____

- _____

Goals: For *each* strategy numbered, outline three or four goals. Make them specific, measurable, and time-bound.

A template for an effective goal statement is *does what by how much by when.* An example from earlier in this chapter is "generate 10 percent market share growth in the next 12 months."

Your goal statement sets a standard, a target for the performance period. Note that your goal statement doesn't say *how* to accomplish the goal; those tactical, day-to-day plans, decisions, and actions must be developed by the team members who will do the work. Don't tell *how* in your strategic plan and goals; tell them *what* the target is.

Paraphrase your strategic imperatives (from point two, earlier), and then add your specific, measurable, time-bound goals for each.

Strategic thrust #1:

_____

_____

Goals (specific, measurable, time-bound):

- _____
- _____
- _____
- _____

Strategic thrust #2:

_____

_____

Goals (specific, measurable, time-bound):

- _____
- _____
- _____
- _____

Strategic thrust #3:

_____

_____

Goals (specific, measurable, time-bound):

- _____
- _____
- _____
- _____

Strategic thrust #4:

_____

_____

Goals (specific, measurable, time-bound):

- _____
- _____
- _____
- _____

Fourth Point: Work

Here you'll map out effective ways to work your plan. What relevant performance dashboards will help communicate progress? How will you communicate, educate, and promote your strategies and goals? How will you align plans, decisions, and actions daily?

Dashboards: _____

_____

_____

_____

Communications strategies: _____

_____

_____

_____

Alignment practices: _____

_____

_____

_____

Fifth Point: Assess

How often will you assess the progress on and effectiveness of your strategies and goals? Who needs to be involved? (Include key players at every level.)

Dashboards: _____

_____

_____

_____

Communications strategies: _____

_____

_____

_____

Alignment practices: _____

_____

_____

_____

The work you've done on this draft strategic plan and goals can serve as a starting point for your discussions with key players on your team or across your company.

Before your first strategic planning session, it would be beneficial for everyone attending to complete his or her draft ideas from this chapter. (And, of course, I'd be honored if you purchased books for all of your key players.)

In your session, as you compare lists and responses, you'll likely find consensus agreement on a number of key elements of your strategic plan and goals. That will accelerate the development of your plan immensely.

When you follow the planning wheel and align daily plans, decisions, and actions to your defined strategic plan, you'll enjoy higher performance, higher-quality results, more engaged team members, and greater customer satisfaction.

Who can argue with those outcomes?

Next we'll examine how to ensure that your organizational constitution is lived by all leaders and team members, every day, in your team or company.

CHAPTER 6

Your Organizational Constitution Must Be LIVED

This chapter explains how leaders must champion their desired culture, every day.

As you've moved through the worksheets in the previous chapters, you have crafted your personal constitution—your purpose, values, and behaviors—as well as your team or company's organizational constitution—its purpose, values, behaviors, strategies, and goals.

This chapter has three main themes that describe the best practices that leaders—culture champions—consistently use to ensure that their organizational constitution is being embraced and lived.

These practices build credibility for both the leaders of the change and the desired change itself.

These themes are:

- **Describe the way**—how leaders must consistently communicate and reinforce their organizational constitution in dozens of ways each week.

- **Model the way**—how leaders must create credibility for their desired culture by their demonstrated alignment to the organization's constitution in every interaction.

- **Align the way**—how leaders must spend time daily observing, assessing, and ensuring alignment of team leaders' and members' interactions and decisions to their organization's constitution.

Keep in mind that the practices we'll describe here are the antidote to the plague of managing by announcements (MbA). We'll not let you announce your organizational constitution and then do nothing further to embed the new practices, processes, or systems.

We know that *the announcement alone* **never** creates the desired change.

This chapter's Culture Effectiveness Assessment gauges the degree to which you, today, align to the three theme's best practices.

Before we dive into our three themes, it's important to clarify the *scope of leadership* of this initiative in your organization.

Culture Effectiveness Assessment #6: Living Your Constitution	Strongly Disagree	Disagree	Slightly Disagree	Slightly Agree	Agree	Strongly Agree
1. **Employee Input on the Organizational Constitution** Employees are given the opportunity to pose questions or make suggestions about the proposed purpose, values, behaviors, strategies, and goals.	1	2	3	4	5	6
2. **Broad Communication of the Organizational Constitution** Once the initial draft is finalized, the organizational constitution is communicated and marketed in a variety of ways—publication, town hall meetings, regular review of values and behaviors, and so on.	1	2	3	4	5	6
3. **Leaders Demonstrate the Organizational Constitution** Leaders are role models of the purpose, values, behaviors, strategies, and goals in every interaction, in all plans, decisions, and actions. The senior leadership team is aligned in its commitment to the desired culture.	1	2	3	4	5	6

Culture Effectiveness Assessment #6: Living Your Constitution	Strongly Disagree	Disagree	Slightly Disagree	Slightly Agree	Agree	Strongly Agree
4. Leaders Invest Time in Observing, Praising, and Coaching Leaders spend more time engaging in discussions and validation of aligned values and behaviors than they do in discussions about performance and goals.	1	2	3	4	5	6
5. Team Members Demonstrate the Organizational Constitution Team members are role models of the purpose, values and behaviors, strategies, and goals in every interaction, in all plans, decisions, and actions.	1	2	3	4	5	6

ENGAGE ALL LEADERS IN YOUR ORGANIZATIONAL CONSTITUTION'S IMPLEMENTATION

As the leader of your team, department, division, or company, you have the authority and responsibility to craft workplace inspiration through an organizational constitution.

If you lead a small team, *you* are the leader who must embrace the culture and champion responsibilities. You don't need anyone else's permission to move forward with your team's organizational constitution. You can begin the culture change process immediately.

In that scenario, the scope of leadership is *you*.

The larger your organization, the larger your sphere of influence or span of control. This increases the number of leaders you must actively engage in the culture refinement initiative.

If you are responsible for a larger organization (i.e., you lead a department),[1] you remain the main champion—you don't need anyone's permission to move forward. And in that scenario the scope of leadership is *you and other formal leaders* of the team, department, division, company, and so on.

And *before* you take your draft organizational constitution to frontline team members, you must engage all those in leadership positions to ensure they have bought into the process.

Engaging your department's next-level leaders becomes your first priority.

You must recruit your department's leaders, managers, and supervisors onto your culture champion team. The best way to recruit them is to walk your leadership team through the three themes.

I know you've been working on your organization's constitution for a while. You're excited about the organizational constitution process! You've mapped out your initial thinking on your department's purpose, values, behaviors, strategies, and goals. But *you can't simply announce your proposed organizational constitution.*

You'll avoid the MbA plague by engaging leaders in conversations about the need for culture refinement in the department.

Before you outline the elements you've drafted in your organizational constitution, you must set the context for the changes you propose.

You must address the question that they're thinking (and maybe that they're asking): "Why culture change and why now?"

The "describe the way" theme will help you set the context for those leaders. You've learned a great deal about how to be intentional about your desired team culture. You need to help your leadership team members learn about organizational constitutions, and help them understand the benefits of a values-aligned work environment.

What's a great way to accelerate their education about organizational constitutions? Purchase this book for each member of your leadership team. Give them time—a couple of weeks or so—to complete their personal constitution and to draft their ideas for the department's organizational constitution.

Before you describe the way, you will educate these leaders with data about the current state of your organization's culture.

Leaders are comfortable with data. They study performance data every day. To these leaders, performance data is undeniable proof of traction on desired output (or lack of desired traction).

It is hoped that, more often than not, they take that performance data and celebrate traction and accomplishment, and coach and redirect where performance falls below standard.

You're going to build these leaders' capability to study and understand data about your department's work environment.

You need to help your leaders see the undeniable proof of the condition of your department's culture today. They need to get comfortable studying data about your department's culture and degree of workplace inspiration.

Over time, you and these leaders will take that culture data and celebrate values traction and alignment, and coach and redirect where values alignment falls below standard. We'll discuss this skill set a bit later in this chapter, in theme three.

By showing them data about how the department's culture operates today, you will help leaders see culture gaps. These leaders need to understand where the department's culture falls short of the characteristics of high-performing, values-aligned organizations.

You'll start by showing them data from *inside* your department, data that provides insights about employees' perceptions of your work environment. You likely have data available that can tell you:

- *Employee satisfaction or engagement.* Surveys, town hall meetings, informal small group meetings with leaders, and so on can provide reliable data about how satisfied employees are with your organization.

- *Absenteeism.* How many days do employees miss work? (This can be a reliable indication of employee dissatisfaction.)

- *Turnover.* How many employees voluntarily leave your department annually?

- *Tenure.* What is the average number of years employees have been with your department? Is the trend rising or shrinking?

- *Time to fill.* How long does it take, on average, to fill open positions in the department?

- *Productivity.* What percentage of performance goals do employees meet or exceed?

- *Revenue per employee.* How much does each employee earn for the department?

There may be additional data available that provide a richer snapshot of employee perceptions of their work environment.

In addition to data from *inside* your organization, educate leaders with data from *outside* your organization that tells them about how employees rate great companies—those that are consistently high performing and values aligned.

I've mentioned a few already: Southwest Airlines, Zappos, WD-40 Company, Starbucks.

Here are a few other high-performing, values-aligned companies worth studying: Asda,[2] Amazon, Ritz-Carlton, Ben & Jerry's, Whole Foods, Quicken Loans, CHG Healthcare.

Many of these organizations are well known; articles and books about their unique organizational culture are readily available. Some are not as well known, but articles about their aligned cultures are within reach, just a web search away.

These are real companies, succeeding in today's global marketplace while boldly stating their values and actively attempting to live by them each day.

What these companies do—deliver high performance *and* values alignment—is possible. It's not only possible but *doable*, using this proven organizational constitution approach.

One other idea will help these leaders understand the need for proactive culture refinement in your department. They need to understand the cost of doing nothing.

Despite all the data you have gathered and reviewed, making a decision to refine your organizational culture might be a difficult one for these leaders to make.

Your inside data shows gaps and issues. The outside data you've studied shows gaps and issues. Your leaders will probably admit that there are ways that the culture could operate better.

And leaders may feel that "it's not so bad, really." They may believe that employee opinions cycle up and down, and there isn't anything to be done about it.

They may be concerned about what the culture change will demand of them, as leaders. They probably do not know *how* to manage their team's culture, since they've likely never done it before.

They may hope the gaps and issues revealed by your data simply go away. They hope they don't have to do anything differently. They hope they can keep on doing what they've always been doing, and everything will be okay.

However, there is a cost of doing nothing.

We've all seen it.

Issues get raised. Promises get made. Yet, *nothing happens*.

One company I know of conducted an employee satisfaction survey and found that employees were overwhelmingly frustrated with policies, leadership, recognition, and compensation. These survey scores were the lowest in the 10-year history of annual employee surveys the company had done.

So, the firm engaged a steering committee made up of senior leaders and middle managers to examine the survey data and map out a strategy for addressing employee concerns.

They met for months. They brought forward any number of ideas and programs to address employee concerns. They debated the pros and cons, the costs, and the time that such programs might require.

Ultimately, they decided to do next to nothing. There was no formal response—not even a published summary of employee rankings from the survey—for nearly 18 months.

When the summary was published, 18 months after the survey was conducted, employees laughed. Their confidence in company leadership was completely eroded.

The programs that were implemented were not effective.

And leadership credibility took such a terrible hit that it took a new leadership team to begin to recover.

It took a year before employee morale and engagement began building again.

Key questions, which you are probably thinking about as you read this, are: Did these leaders think employees didn't *know* that morale was so bad? Did they think that ignoring the survey for 18 months would improve employee perceptions?

Employees talk. They're very open about the issues they see, the challenges they face, and the leadership issues they experience. They have opinions.

They don't miss a thing.

Once you gather your inside data and examine the issues you face—like absenteeism, turnover, productivity, and quality—you can't turn back the clock and unlearn what that culture data has shown you.

The issues and gaps exist—in every organization on the planet.

Trying to hide the culture gaps you've discovered under a bushel basket will not make those gaps go away. Nor will ignoring these gaps reduce their negative impact on employee performance and employee engagement.

It is hoped that you and your leadership team will come to this same conclusion: the team must address the culture gaps. They can't ignore those gaps; the costs are too great.

Do *all* of the leaders in your department have to be in *complete agreement* with the culture refinement initiative?

Many of those leaders will have concerns. Some will have real fears of what you're proposing. As we noted a few pages ago, these leaders have never engaged in a culture change before! They've likely never lived in a work environment where values alignment is as important as output and results.

You won't start with 100 percent engagement from your department leadership team, but your goal is to gain 100 percent *willingness to try*.

You want their active support in the organizational constitution process.

Over time, your desired work environment will take shape, behaving in alignment with your organizational constitution. These changes will help many of your leaders gain confidence that this is a better way to run the business.

A few may not be quite as confident, engaged, or willing right at the start. This is natural and to be expected. And you can't tolerate leaders who are only "kind of" on board with the culture refinement. You need leaders who are fully on board, willing to modify their behavior and interactions to model and coach alignment to the way.

We'll discuss strategies for dealing with resistance from leaders and team members in more detail in Chapter 8.

Once your department's leadership team is engaged, you and the leadership team will engage the rest of your organization in the three themes.

DESCRIBE THE WAY

This first theme is about communication and marketing of your desired culture, of the elements of your organizational constitution. Before engaging in the culture marketing campaign, you must first engage all staff in reviewing the initial, draft version of your organizational constitution.

Remember that, at this point, you've been actively involved in thinking about your organizational constitution, drafting your organizational constitution, and helping your leadership team members gain context and comfort with implementing an organizational constitution.

You know the specifics of your draft business purpose, values, behaviors, strategies, and goals very well. You know these elements better than your leadership team members know them!

Your employees are starting from scratch. They have not had the opportunity to even consider these elements, much less immerse themselves in crafting these elements.

You'll begin describing the way by sharing the constitution in draft form. The word *draft* is important to use. You don't want to distribute a pretty version on company letterhead at this stage, because then the constitution looks like it's done.

If it looks like it's done, and someone with a position of authority presents it, employees will think the organizational constitution is done.

That'll feel a lot like an outbreak of MbA, won't it?

Print the constitution on plain paper. Put a watermark on each page that says "DRAFT" in big, light gray letters, something like this:

A watermark will help emphasize that the constitution is truly in draft form. It has been thought through, but it's in need of employee input and validation. It'll be ready for publication only after employees see it, consider it, and provide suggestions for improving it.

Leave space on each page for all employees (including managers, team leads, supervisors, and frontline staff) to note their questions or suggestions for making the behaviors more specific or measurable. For example:

Proposed Values and Valued Behaviors

What do you think? What are we missing? How can we be more specific about the behaviors we want everyone to demonstrate with this value?

Value: Integrity

Definition: We make promises intentionally and keep our commitments religiously. We do what we say we will do.

Behavior #1: I always deliver on my promises. If for any reason it looks like I will miss a deadline, I let all stakeholders know in advance what I can do and my suggestions to mitigate any issues.

Set the context and describe what the proposed organizational constitution means. What does the draft purpose mean? What do the values and behaviors mean—to every individual in the department? What do the performance strategies and goals mean?

It's likely that employees will be most comfortable with your strategies and goals. These will likely be very familiar to team members because they'll commonly align with your existing performance metrics and dashboards.

You may be adding some new performance standards in your strategies and goals, but it's unlikely that these performance declarations will generate much concern. They'll make sense, since you have (probably) already been talking about these targets.

The purpose, values, and valued behaviors just might generate questions, concerns, and enthusiasm!

Point out that you've got great department citizens today. Your organizational constitution is intended to clarify and formalize how great team citizens act, so that everyone—leaders, employees, everyone—can embrace the valued behaviors.

You might even share the performance-values matrix on a chart pad. That model will help team members understand how you're not changing your focus on performance; you're adding a focus on team citizenship and values to complement the performance required by the team.

Emphasize that these new guidelines (values, behaviors, etc.) will be required of everyone in the department—eventually. Explain that formal leaders, managers, and supervisors will be asked to model them *first*.

Leaders of people will embrace these new liberating rules immediately. Let team members know that they will be surveyed approximately six months after the final draft organizational constitution is published. That values survey will ask employees to rate their bosses on how well their bosses model the purpose, values, behaviors, and so on. (We'll learn more about gathering feedback about values alignment in Chapter 7.)

Point out the space on the draft constitution where you want their input. Formally ask for and invite their comments, feedback, and edits over a short, specific time frame. Give them a two-week window to make their suggestions and turn them in.

You might create a mailbox where suggestions can be emailed. Some team members might prefer writing their ideas, edits, additions, and the like on the paper draft you've distributed. Offer as many easy feedback avenues as team members need.

It is likely that most employees will offer no input. That's okay. It's important to open the door to their involvement right here, at the start of your culture refinement process.

Once the two-week feedback deadline has passed, review suggested edits and enhancements. Formally thank employees for their feedback. Tell them you are actively reviewing their input and will submit the final draft in no more than two weeks.

You and the leadership team decide which suggestions make sense and are ones that you all support. Add them to the elements of your organizational constitution.

Then publish and communicate your final draft constitution as a set of guidelines for how all leaders in the department will behave.

Yes, you can publish it on company letterhead. Just note "final draft" and the date published on each page.

Explain that it's a final draft that may, as you all learn how the draft values and behaviors (for example) work from day to day, be revised—as needed—in a couple of years.

Reiterate that, now that the new liberating rules have been formalized and published, department leaders will be asked to demonstrate these elements daily. They'll be required to model these values and behaviors in every interaction, with employees, with customers, even with strangers (!).

Invite team members to align to these values and behaviors, as well. They'll model these behaviors if they see their leaders living these behaviors.

They won't model them if leaders don't model them.

The final element of the "describe the way" theme is to embark on a consistent marketing campaign for your business purpose and values.

It is less important to campaign on the strategic plan and goals. Your established and newly implemented performance metrics, dashboards, and the like will ensure that goal traction is closely monitored.

The new elements—purpose, values, and valued behaviors—need regular reinforcement to embed them in the daily normal interactions within and across your department.

The campaign will include visible signs of the purpose, values, and behaviors. Create posters and place them around your department. Start meetings with recognition of terrific values-aligned plans, decisions, and actions.

Hold all-department meetings at least monthly. Feature—and celebrate – stories and examples of values alignment at the start of those meetings. Yes, you'll review performance metrics and financial results as well. The difference now is that you'll be placing purpose and values up on the same pedestal as performance and profits.

Ritz-Carlton is known the world over for its exceptional customer service. It built a service-focused organization by crafting its "Gold Standards,"[3] which include its credo, its motto, the three steps of service, the 12 service values, the 6th diamond, and the employee promise. This is Ritz-Carlton's organizational constitution, and the company aligns plans, decisions, and actions to it daily.

One of Ritz-Carlton's marketing strategies for its Gold Standards is a daily 15-minute all-employee meeting, called a "lineup." The primary focus of these meetings is storytelling—specifically, telling the "wow story" of the day detailing a staff member's outstanding customer service efforts to create the Ritz-Carlton mystique for a guest.

The same "wow story" is told each day in every Ritz-Carlton around the globe. These stories not only honor the efforts of a staff member but also reinforce one of the service values (a different one each day).

These stories inspire employees to find their own unique ways of wowing their guests—and these stories reinforce the Ritz-Carlton's desired service culture.

One of my culture clients held quarterly all-hands meetings. Those used to be boring sessions where leaders would read performance results and maybe celebrate a long-term employee's anniversary every once in a while.

When they published their organizational constitution, leaders realized that these meetings could be (1) more frequent to boost effective communications, and (2) more inspiring for employees.

They shifted to monthly all-hands meetings. And they invited employees to present engaging ways of celebrating the plant's new purpose, values, and behaviors.

A volunteer committee made up of employees from around the facility organized the presentations. Frontline staff delivered the presentations, as well.

I attended one all-hands meeting where the employee presentation was on safety. Instead of a typical dry reading of safety guidelines, the committee had taken photographs of unsafe practices followed by photographs of safe practices.

The photos featured frontline team members, well known to the employees at the plant. The audience roared with laughter at a "before," unsafe example picture of a peer on her hands and knees picking up spilled materials while a fellow employee sat inches away with his feet up on the desk, reading the sports page!

The "after," safe practices photo showed the sports fan on the floor, side by side with his teammate, picking up the spilled materials, too.

Many of us are visual learners. We learn more and retain more when we see examples of aligned practices than we do listening to someone tell us about aligned practices.

Regular meetings, team discussions, storytelling, and visual snapshots can be an effective part of your purpose and values marketing campaign.

A very important element of the purpose, values, and behaviors campaign is every leader's personal commitment to living them. Each leader must invite feedback from his or her team members. The leader needs to open the door wide and make it safe for employees to provide this feedback, and needs to encourage this feedback.

The fastest way to embed these values and behaviors into daily practice by all leaders and team members is to make them a part of daily conversations. Leaders, it's up to you to ensure that those conversations happen!

MODEL THE WAY

Once the organizational constitution has been published, leaders must model the valued behaviors, every day, in every interaction.

These new valued behaviors describe how a great team citizen (or department citizen) looks, acts, and sounds.

They also define the singular path that leaders must walk. Imagine an overgrown field. The ground is uneven. Footing is difficult, and walking is nearly impossible. Now imagine a freshly paved walkway through the field. It is much easier to move through the field while walking the paved path!

That's what defined valued behaviors do—they smooth the desired path through uneven territory.

If leaders stray off that path, for any reason, and do not model the valued behaviors as defined, they're telling fellow department members, "I don't care about our values or behaviors."

Let's consider an example. Say that one of your department's valued behaviors is "I do what I say I will do," part of your integrity value.

Leaders must be more intentional with their commitments now. They need to be very clear about what they promise to do, and by when. A leader may make a commitment to his team by saying, "When we complete this project on time and under budget, I'm taking everyone out to lunch to celebrate."

That's a formal commitment. It's a promise made publicly and boldly.

In order for that leader to do what he said he would do, he'll need to make sure that recognition lunch happens, and it happens well, for everyone on the team.

If the project completion happens on time and on budget with no mention of a celebratory lunch, everyone on the team will think, "Our boss lied to us. He isn't going to take us to lunch after all."

The leader's credibility is eroded, immediately.

Even his future commitments will be viewed from a place of "Oh, well, here's another promise that will be broken."

When the celebratory lunch isn't mentioned, the leader should expect that he will get called on it. Fellow leaders will call him out first (if they know about the missed commitment). In this case, you'd want the team members to engage the leader and say, "We met our part of the bargain. Where are we going to lunch, like you promised?"

Some leaders may feel that this scrutiny is harsh and unfair. They may feel that team members will look for any chink in their armor so they can discount leaders and discount this effort.

It may be harsh and unfair, but it is the reality of a culture refinement. Leaders have to lead and model this charge.

Employees will not only scrutinize leader behaviors *inside* the work environment but will do so *outside*, as well.

I tell leaders all the time, "You'll never be able to run a yellow light in this town again."

You won't be able to cut in line at the movie theater again.

You won't be able to take 11 items through the "10 items or fewer" express lane at the grocery store.

And—this scrutiny is a good thing. It will help leaders keep their focus on modeling the defined department values and behaviors.

Don't give leaders or employees the ability to opt out of living by the new rules of your organizational constitution.

Don't think, though, that this transition will be a piece of cake. It won't.

The organizational constitution demands different behaviors and different thought processes by leaders.

Leaders will have to break habits formed over years (possibly even over decades) so they align with the new department purpose, values, behaviors, strategies, and goals.

We're all human—even your leaders are human. They'll make mistakes.

Making mistakes isn't the problem. Trying to gloss over mistakes, misaligned behaviors, and the like is the problem.

When you miss the mark, own your mistake. Apologize promptly. Say, "I'm better than that. It won't happen again."

Leaders need to share their intentions (to model their department's purpose, values, and behaviors) and share their learnings with team members. The leaders' insights on their own "values transition" can be very helpful to team members as they learn to embrace the organizational constitution, as well.

ALIGN THE WAY

Once leaders embrace their responsibility to demonstrate the department's values and behaviors, leaders must then coach other leaders, managers, supervisors, and so on (anyone with formal direct reports) to demonstrate the valued behaviors as well.

Don't assume that someone else will have the needed alignment conversations. Often leaders hope that the most senior leader will "do that alignment stuff."

That's not how it works! Every leader needs to engage in these alignment conversations—the positive reinforcement of aligned behaviors as well as the redirection of misaligned behaviors.

Every interaction with a peer, a team member, or a customer brings an opportunity for aligned behavior by leaders or for misaligned behavior.

Leaders have to be consciously intentional with values alignment, every minute. Old habits die hard, and regressing to previous norms is tempting.

The same can be said for team members. Before they'll invest in being consciously intentional with your valued behaviors, they must be shown that their leaders are fully invested in those behaviors.

"Align the way" means that there are consequences for behaviors—positive consequences for aligned behaviors, and negative consequences for misaligned behaviors.

Negative consequences don't mean immediate suspension or firing. That's too strong a reaction! Negative consequences likely mean a private discussion and one-on-one coaching. That's an appropriate first level of negative consequences, bringing awareness of the misaligned behavior and agreement on how to align the leader's behavior.

"Align the way" means leaders are vigilant, observing their fellow leaders, managers, and supervisors. They are consistent with praising the demonstration of desired valued behaviors and redirecting the demonstration of undesired behaviors.

When trying to create consistent workplace inspiration, leaders need to praise, encourage, and reinforce desired behaviors nine times as frequently as they zing people for misaligned behavior. Leverage and deepen the understanding of what you want people to do; that will pull them toward doing those behaviors more willingly and frequently.

Alignment also opens the door to refining old systems, policies, and procedures to encourage desired valued behaviors—not performance at any cost.

CONTRIBUTION MANAGEMENT INSTEAD OF PERFORMANCE MANAGEMENT

With your organizational constitution in place, you need to align systems, policies, and procedures to your new liberating rules and expectations.

Many companies are dissatisfied with their existing performance management process. Some are radically changing their systems to include more feedback more often, and to include feedback on values and fit.

In a recent *Forbes* article about this trend, Josh Bersin suggests that giving leaders "a cultural framework and set of values to work from" requires leaders to "hire and manage to these values." It enables leaders to "coach people against higher level frameworks."[4]

I don't think a radical change is necessary. I suggest a *refinement* of your performance management process. First, call it "contribution management." That term better defines what you're looking for—equal contributions of performance *and* values alignment by every leader and team member in your organization.

First, ensure that the performance side of the equation is solid. Your strategic plan outlines department goals and probably team goals. Those team goals and related individual goals need to be formalized in each leader's and team member's contribution plan.

Make the goal expectations specific, measurable, and trackable. Make sure they have a deadline for completion (goals without a deadline are probably activities, which are much less valuable to formalize and spend time on in your plan).

And, in this fast-paced, global marketplace we live in, goals change quickly. That's okay. Use your contribution plan to keep track of goals that are completed, goals that are set aside, new goals that are added, and so on. That'll probably require regular updating of this plan.

Good! It's important to keep the plan current and relevant.

Then, ensure that the valued behaviors side of the equation is solid. You'll use the behaviors from your values statement as a foundation for these citizenship metrics.

Make your values expectations specific, measurable, and trackable. These behaviors will not have a deadline since you want everyone to demonstrate them every day.

We'll look at ways of gathering valid data about values alignment in the next chapter. This data can be folded into every player's contribution appraisal at year-end (or every six months, etc., however your contribution assessment cycle works).

Some clients have gone into greater detail with evaluating values alignment in their contribution appraisal process. They've taken the valued behaviors and defined three levels of values demonstration: exceeds standard, meets standard, and needs improvement.

Here are one client's three degrees of valued behaviors for the value of "make and keep commitments."

Exceeds Standard

- Commits to his or her commitments by putting key commitments down in writing and sharing that document with stakeholders in that commitment.

- When unable to commit for any reason, expresses that inability clearly.

- When unable to keep a commitment, informs all key stakeholders promptly.

- Holds team members accountable for commitments they have made to him or her and to related internal customers.

Meets Standard

- Willing to put commitments in writing if asked.

- Works hard to deliver on promises made, though deadlines are missed on occasion.

- Attempts to keep key stakeholders informed if deadline is to be missed.

- Struggles to express desire to hold team members accountable for commitments they've made.

Needs Improvement

- Difficult to pin down on commitments for key projects. Unwilling to put commitments in writing.

- Though he or she may commit to deadlines, he or she misses those performance deadlines more often than not.

- Sees role of "holding people accountable" as his or her manager's problem.

- Complains loudly when team members miss deadlines or commitments to him or her.

These observable, behavioral definitions of this client's "make and keep commitments" value help its leaders give actionable feedback to their direct reports. If their team members are not at the "exceeds standard" level, the leader can coach to the specific behaviors that are desired.

THE VALUES-ALIGNED TRIBE CULTURE AT WD-40 COMPANY

What could be better than to end this chapter with a client's values-alignment success story?

Garry Ridge is president and CEO of WD-40 Company. We met when he joined the first cohort class of the Master of Science in Executive Leadership (MSEL) program at the University of San Diego in 2000. I was a faculty member of that program for 10 years, and Garry was seeking his master's degree in leadership.

I interviewed Garry recently to learn more about why he chose to refine the culture of a successful public company, how he did it, and what impact the values journey has had on the business, on the company's team members, and on the company's customers.

Garry joined WD-40 Company in 1987 as managing director of the Australia subsidiary, one of the company's first attempts at global reach and global branding. At that time the company was very U.S.-centric. WD-40 Company's revenues were $80 million (U.S. dollars) with $60 million of that total coming from U.S. sales.

In those days the company's U.S.-centric mind-set included a highly command-and-control culture. Decisions were made autocratically in the United States from a U.S. point of view. Garry realized that if the company were to extend its brand globally, that mind-set had to change.

When Garry was made CEO in 1997, WD-40 Company was a successful U.S. brand. It was not yet a successful global brand—but it had the potential to become one. Garry believed that if he could help the company's leaders create a people infrastructure that supported a global brand, they could realize and exceed that potential.

Today, WD-40 is a $330 million global brand—and about 65 percent of sales come from outside the United States. The growth of the organization is a testament to Garry's instincts and to the people he has engaged in the WD-40 Company tribe.

Garry noted that in 1997, "The currency of the day was information. The more I had and the less I shared, the more power I had. WD-40 Company was a very siloed organization back then."

If WD-40 Company was to grow as a global brand, the company couldn't do it by being a U.S.-focused, information-hoarding culture.

Though Garry had been with the company for more than 10 years at that point, he was an outsider; he wasn't a part of the existing, U.S.-centric leadership team.

"Why would U.S.-centric leadership put an Australian with a limited understanding of how the U.S. public company system works in charge of WD-40 Company? They knew their future success lay in global growth and felt an insider wouldn't be able to lead that global branding effort," Garry said. The leaders of the company believed they had the perfect man in Garry to drive global growth.

In the MSEL program, Ken and Margie Blanchard helped students craft their leadership point of view (LPOV). Garry had an epiphany while crafting his. He explained, "There is a corporate leadership point of view, too. The corporate LPOV can only evolve as key leaders' LPOV evolves."

What is WD-40 Company's corporate leadership point of view today? Garry said, "First, micromanagement is not scalable! If WD-40 Company was to spread their brand around the world, they needed to craft a work environment that treasures learning and teaching, fairness, candor, mutual respect, trust, perseverance, fun, and had to try to do it globally."

Garry knew that creating that safe, inspiring work environment would take intent and action by the company's leaders. And it would take time for that shift to occur.

Garry asked himself, "What's stopping people from sharing the information they have?" He spoke to people around the company and discovered that the answer was fear of failure.

Garry decided, right then and there, that he'd remove *failure* from the company's vocabulary. He'd replace it with *learning moment*. This was one of Garry's first significant aha moments regarding the WD-40 Company culture. He decided that WD-40 Company people would no longer have failures; they'd have learning moments, which he defines as a positive or negative outcome of any situation.

Humans are prone to hide their failures. Garry helped his team members to embrace their own learning moments and to share them, openly and freely, around the organization. That way, everyone can benefit from positive or negative learning moments!

Garry began embedding the learning moment language in the company starting in about 2001. He spent a year asking people around the company to share their learning.

Garry's MSEL experiences built his confidence in his beliefs that this was the right direction to go: to help WD-40 Company become a learning organization with sustained growth. MSEL also helped shift Garry's thinking about the possibility of creating a tribe environment at WD-40 Company.

Garry began studying tribes, including Aboriginal tribe behaviors. Their first tribal attribute is identity and belonging; their second attribute is learning and teaching. Both of those attributes were needed in the evolving WD-40 Company culture, Garry thought.

Garry then adapted Abraham Maslow's Hierarchy of Needs to his organization. In the needs pyramid, the basic, foundational needs are physiological and safety needs. Garry felt the learning moment shifts were already helping with those needs. The pyramid's third level described the need for belonging, which aligned perfectly to his growing understanding of tribal cultures.

This was Garry's second aha moment regarding the evolving WD-40 Company culture: people need to feel as though they're *wanted* and they *belong* in WD-40 Company.

Garry explained, "Companies don't typically embrace belonging. They see it as soft and not relevant to hard dollars and results."

Belonging has other desirable attributes in organizations. Garry said, "I think I belong if I'm being developed, if I'm making a genuine contribution, if I'm being respected." He knew the company needed to formalize the values he wanted those in the organization to live.

He brought in Ken Blanchard to spend one Sunday afternoon with the top 25 WD-40 Company leaders from around the globe. Ken helped the team focus on their most desirable values. Over the next six months Garry and his team continued to craft their values, definitions, and behaviors. They socialized the values with WD-40 Company team members around the world to assess alignment and agreement.

During this time Garry realized that some members of his leadership team weren't fully invested. Some thought Garry was "drinking the Kool-Aid" of this values stuff. They weren't boldly resisting, but it was obvious. Garry engaged these few players in conversations and gave them a chance to embrace the new way.

If any leadership team members couldn't fully engage in this culture transition, Garry invited those players to find somewhere else to work. He said, "I told them we're not giving up on this. This will become more uncomfortable for you. I told them it was time for them to go."

As the company's vision and values evolved—and the leadership team evolved—Garry asked WD-40 Company leaders to fully embrace the tribal culture. "Our leaders need to say, 'I'm not here to mark your paper—I'm here to help you get an A,'" he said. (You might enjoy Garry's book with Ken Blanchard on this topic.[5])

WD-40 Company leaders must embrace the company's vision and values and "engage our people. Managers need to help their tribe members to step into the best version of their best self—and outline how they're going to do it," Garry explained.

WD-40 Company's values and tribal culture are embedded in every investor communication. "It starts with culture, people, work environment, beliefs, and values—then we cover the financials," said Garry.

When looking at an organization's culture, the most important player is the team member. Soon after Garry's selection as

CEO, the company employed an employee feedback system that continues today.

Every two years, WD-40 Company employees complete a survey that ranks their degree of engagement—how delighted they are with the WD-40 Company work environment, with their leaders, and with their peers.

"Today, 93.7 percent of WD-40 Company employees say they are engaged," said Garry, proudly.

Fully 98 percent of tribe members participated in the company's 2014 survey. The five highest-rated items by employees were:

1. I understand how my job contributes to achieving WD-40 Company goals. (99.7 percent favorable)

2. I know what results are expected of me. (98.6 percent favorable)

3. I love to tell people that I work for WD-40 Company. (97.9 percent favorable)

4. I am clear on the company's goals. (97.1 percent favorable)

5. I respect my supervisor. (97.1 percent favorable)

Garry is rightfully pleased with these engagement scores. They are some of the highest I've seen from any culture client.

And—engaged employees produce like the dickens.

As engagement scores have grown since 1997, so has growth in annual revenues and in returns to shareholders. "There is an absolute correlation of growth across those three vital areas," Garry reported.

Garry believes that the company's vision, values, and tribal culture create "positive lasting memories for the users of our products, our tribe members, and our shareholders."

The issue for many organizations is that although they leave lasting memories on customers, staff, and shareholders, they're just not consistently *positive* memories!

Garry knows that the biggest reason why people leave organizations is a lousy relationship with their boss. Why? "Leaders are not helping people feel like they belong," he explained.

WD-40 Company's values and tribal culture are fully embedded in its talent review system, in communications, in the employee opinion survey, and in day-to-day practices.

"In tribe meetings, tribe members sit down and share how each has lived the values in the last nine days. There are only two places to go with our values: lived or visited," Garry related, "and we don't tolerate visiting the values here."

"We've lost some players because they've not lived the values," Garry confessed. "We 'share them with the competition'!" He has let very visible players go when their values were not aligned to the company's culture. The values are a key part of the company's tribal environment. He says, "We continue to communicate it, celebrate it, and coach it."

Garry described the importance of the company's global tribal council—the core leadership team. "Language is very important," he related. In the company's tribal culture, there is no better term for the top leadership team than *global tribal council*.

That team, Garry explains, must be aligned, "not only to the company's vision, values, and culture, but to the council's mission: 'to create an enduring company we'd be proud to pass on to others.'"

The global tribal council has no right to make people miserable. If that occurs, "Bad on us," Garry said.

The council's golden rule is they can vibrantly debate ideas in the conference room, but the team is totally aligned on decisions when they leave that conference room. "If a tribal council member discounts a council decision, they're voted off the island!" Garry declared.

When the council is discussing any decision or opportunity, Garry described the way they ensure they are honoring the company's values and constituent groups. "We post the opportunity or decision on a chart," he said, "and list the values down the side and our three constituent groups—shareholders, tribe members, and consumers—across the top of the chart." They assess the decision from the perspective of every value and every constituency. If they find any negative impact, they can't move forward.

This approach started with the global tribal council and is now embraced by the whole company. "Even junior account managers pose questions like these," Garry reported. "It happens daily."

For example, WD-40 Company uses no ingredient that's known to cause cancer in any company product. "We've walked away from millions of dollars' worth of business," Garry explained. "Other companies do it, but we just walk away."

During the global recession, "we never laid off one person," Garry said. Tribes band together more closely during stressful times.

Garry believes that creating and maintaining the right culture takes time. "There are many variables you must manage. There is no silver bullet," he said.

Garry is grateful that his board, shareholders, and tribe members gave him the time—and continue to give him the time—to make the transformation to a tribal culture.

"People like the WD-40 Company culture. As the culture gets stronger, it spits out people who are not values aligned," Garry explained. People are knocking the door down to join the company. "There's a great, positive buzz out there. People know about our great culture. We have people come in every day who tell us, 'I have to work for the WD-40 Company!'" Garry said.

"There's nothing like the freedom of a clearly defined goal and clearly defined values," Garry exclaimed. When WD-40 Company leaders pay attention to the things that matter to their people, then people will be fulfilled in their jobs. "When people are fulfilled, they do the right things to serve customers. When fulfilled people serve customers, growth happens."

As we closed our interview, Garry said, "You can't create an enduring company that creates positive memories without inspired team members. That's the job that leaders have to do well: inspire team members every day."

Garry Ridge is excited about the WD-40 Company's future. He's crafted a safe, inspiring tribal culture that creates positive memories *every day* for customers, tribe members, and shareholders.

Along this culture journey, Garry and the tribal leaders at WD-40 Company described the way, modeled the way, and aligned the way.

If a siloed, information-hoarding, command-and-control culture can be refined using these approaches, they just might work with your team or department.

CHAPTER 7

Gathering Formal Feedback on Valued Behaviors

The difference between leaders who successfully implement an organizational constitution and those who don't boils down to one vitally important practice: accountability.

Let's start with your experiences with performance accountability. How do you hold team members accountable, today, for their performance commitments?

In the best systems, goals are defined during performance planning for each team member. Those goals are aligned to the strategic plan of the department (again, we're using department as an example because these practices are scalable to larger divisions, plants, etc.).

These goals are defined in specific, measurable, and trackable terms. The goal statement itself outlines specific and measurable targets, how and when those targets will be measured, and when those goals must be delivered.

Once the planning portion is complete, work on those goals begins. While team members apply their time, energy, and skills toward meeting (or exceeding) formalized goals, the leader takes on the role of performance observer and coach.

The observer role happens before the coaching role begins. Leaders must gather information about performance progress from many channels—from their own observations, from the team member, from their team, from performance dashboards and metrics, from the customer, and so on.

NUTTERISMS

"I BELIEVE YOU BELIEVE THAT."

If you believe one thing and I believe another, we may never find common ground—and may struggle to work together.

I will get accurate, reliable data, and review it, and then share insights and educate others on the realities as I see them. If I do that well, we can move forward and contribute together.

Leaders can't depend on only one source. They must tap numerous reliable sources to ensure they're getting an accurate overall picture of performance to standard by their team members.

In the coaching role, leaders share the performance traction they've observed from their various channels. As needed, the leader can provide skill building to get the goal back on track, or engage with the team member in problem solving, or praise and encourage the team member, or simply say, "You're right on it. Is there anything you need from me to deliver this goal as promised?"

Where performance is off track, the leader engages in coaching, teaching, and guiding to get team member performance back on track.

Where performance is on track, the leader validates the team member's efforts and accomplishment. The leader praises, encourages, and delegates responsibility to the team member who is performing well. The leader engages in discussion with the team member about exceeding performance standards where possible.

At their core, these planning, observing, and coaching activities enable the leader to help each team member deliver on his or her performance expectations.

This is performance accountability in action. Performance accountability works well when there are:

- Clear agreements about goal expectations
- Accurate observations of progress

- Relevant coaching and recognition of effort and accomplishment
- Redirection where needed to regain performance traction
- Celebration of performance delivery to agreed-to standards

That's the best scenario. But it's all too rare in today's fast-paced business environments.

What is a more typical scenario?

Some of my clients struggle with goal clarity and clear agreements. Leaders don't do enough observation from various channels. They may not have the time to do so. Or they may not believe they need to take that time—"I've got self-directed team members. They're on it!"

Employees believe that relevant coaching, praising, or redirection is infrequent. Team members tell me they think their bosses set performance targets and then *hope* that team members get them done.

If you don't know it yet, I can tell you without reservation: *Hope is not a sustainable strategy!*

Maybe your performance accountability practices are nearer to the first scenario than the second one. Maybe you can take some of these techniques and apply them with your team members to boost performance accountability, now.

This chapter isn't about performance accountability. It's about values accountability—and I'll outline how you can use the same best practices we just outlined to boost values demonstration.

In high-performance, values-aligned organizations, values accountability is of equal importance with performance accountability. Leaders spend as much time, if not more, communicating, modeling, and reinforcing the department's values and valued behaviors.

Leaders spend more time on values accountability because systems exist already to monitor and reinforce performance expectations. Because values expectations are typically new to the organization, leaders must invest time and energy crafting systems to monitor and reinforce values expectations.

This chapter's Culture Effectiveness Assessment gauges how well your current team or company uses the proven best practices of values feedback and accountability today.

The best practice system for values accountability includes the same elements as those we just discussed for performance accountability.

Culture Effectiveness Assessment #7: Values Feedback	Strongly Disagree	Disagree	Slightly Disagree	Slightly Agree	Agree	Strongly Agree
1. Values Agreements Every organization member has formally committed to modeling the defined values and behaviors.	1	2	3	4	5	6
2. Values Reinforcement The team's purpose, values, and behaviors are discussed regularly. Stories are frequently told that celebrate values demonstration.	1	2	3	4	5	6
3. Values Alignment Is Embedded in Reviews Leaders and team members have specific values expectations spelled out in their performance plans.	1	2	3	4	5	6
4. Values Perceptions Are Formally Gathered A custom values survey is conducted at least once per year. Leaders receive a values profile that includes overall team data as well as data from their functional team.	1	2	3	4	5	6
5. Leaders Act on Values Feedback Leaders embrace feedback from the values survey data and from day-to-day perceptions. They refine their plans, decisions, and actions to align to their team's purpose, values, and behaviors.	1	2	3	4	5	6

If performance goals are the "what" a team member delivers, values expectations outline "how" a team member will interact with others in the course of their day-to-day work.

Both the "what" and the "how" need to be explicitly defined and formalized.

In the contribution-planning phase, values expectations outline what great team member citizenship looks like. Values are defined in specific, measurable, and trackable behaviors. This approach ensures that both the leader and team member agree to the minimum standards for great team citizenship.

Once the planning portion is complete, work on both performance goals and valued behaviors begins. While team members apply their time, energy, and skills toward meeting (or exceeding) formalized goals in ways that model the team's values, the leader takes on the role of values observer and coach.

As with performance observation, the observer role happens before the coaching role begins. Leaders must gather information about values alignment from many channels—from their own observations, from the team member, from their team, from the custom values survey, from their customers, and so on.

Leaders can't depend on only one source to assess the values match. They must tap numerous reliable sources to ensure they're getting an accurate overall picture of values alignment by their team member.

What is different from performance coaching is that values coaching typically happens more frequently. Some performance goals are for long time frames—weeks or months. Values coaching may be needed on a weekly or even daily basis.

In the coaching role, the leader shares the values feedback gathered from various channels. If the team member is viewed as modeling desired valued behaviors, the leader validates the team member's values alignment. The leader can simply say, "You're right on it. Is there anything you need from me to continue modeling our values?"

If the team member is *not* viewed as modeling desired valued behaviors, the leader must engage in coaching and redirection to address the values gap. The leader must present the observed behavior and compare it to desired valued behavior.

The leader doesn't allow the team member to behave in ways that are inconsistent with the stated valued behaviors. The leader must inspire values alignment in the team member—or the leader must deal proactively with a misaligned team member.

At their core, values planning, observing, and coaching activities enable the leader to help each team member deliver expected performance (the "what") while demonstrating desired valued behaviors (the "how").

This is values accountability in action! Values accountability works well when there are:

- Clear agreements about values expectations
- Accurate observation and evaluation of values demonstration
- Relevant coaching and recognition of values demonstration
- Redirection where needed to regain expected citizenship
- Celebration of values alignment

That's the best scenario for managing values alignment. As we've noted, values expectations and values accountability are extremely rare in today's fast-paced business environments.

Shifting to values accountability will generate some interesting reactions from your leaders, managers, and supervisors.

Most organizations have approached policy changes with a managing by announcements (MbA) mind-set. The changes would be announced, leaders would hope people would align to them, and little more would be done.

You've engaged people in your department with crafting and refining your business values and behaviors. You've engaged people in agreeing to demonstrate your new values and behaviors.

That's important, foundational work for your desired culture change. And, in essence, the values and behaviors have been announced. Now you're shifting to *real, live values accountability*. And people will typically react in one of four ways.

In the first way, some people (leaders, managers, supervisors, and team members) will embrace the values and behaviors thoroughly. Their reaction will be one of "Well, shoot. I can easily model these valued behaviors! Why didn't you ask me before?"

More people than you might expect will react in this fashion. You'd naturally expect your benchmark citizens to embrace the values and behaviors promptly, but it's also likely that a bunch of your players will engage willingly in modeling your stated values and behaviors.

As noted earlier, you'll build credibility for values alignment when your leaders model, coach, and reinforce the values and behaviors. Leaders who are legitimate culture champions will help greater numbers of players in your department to embrace your values and behaviors.

The second reaction is "wait and see." This is a passive approach. These players have seen many policy changes come and go. They're used to MbA. They simply hope this values thing is just another example of that—a passing fad.

These players will periodically try out the values and behaviors but only when coached or directed to do so. They'd rather sit on the sidelines and do nothing to attract attention to themselves. They'll wait and see how this change plays out.

The third reaction to values accountability is for players to self-select out of the department. This is an assertive reaction. They choose to leave rather than engage in trying the values and behaviors.

They might think, "I've never been asked to do this before. It has never been important before, and I don't think it's worth my time or energy today. I'm out."

Or they might think, "You're not paying me more money to do this values stuff. I'd rather go transfer to a different department or to a different facility or to a different company where I can just do my performance thing."

The fourth reaction is "stay and resist." This is a passive-aggressive approach. These players do not agree with the shift to values and behaviors. Rather than leave, though, they choose to stay and fight.

They're not below the radar—they're in your face! They are open with their disagreement with this change.

They poke fun at those who embrace the values and behaviors. They roll their eyes at discussions of purpose, values, and behaviors. They even share their frustrations with customers.

They are bold with their dissent. They are firmly in the camp of "This values stuff is horse manure."

They are confident that nothing will happen to them. After all, the department has announced other policy changes in the past and nothing really changed. They feel secure in their resistance!

Each one of these reactions requires an intentional response. If leaders do nothing, your organizational constitution will feel like a flavor of the month.

Leaders must invest time and energy daily in praising, validating, and reinforcing those players who embrace the purpose, values, and behaviors.

Leaders must push and prod those who are passively observing from the sidelines. Doing nothing with values alignment must not be tolerated. Leaders need to shrink the number of players in this "wait and see" group—as quickly as possible. You would prefer that they embrace the values and join the first reaction group. If they're unable to do that, you will help them decide to leave the organization. You will lovingly set them free because you cannot tolerate values misalignment—even by top performers!

Leaders must thank those who choose to leave the company, praising them for their past contributions. Lovingly set them free without malice and without judgment. (How you set people free says a lot about your values. Be nice, be kind—and move on.)

Leaders must push and prod those who are actively resisting the purpose, values, and behaviors. When these players act out, passively or aggressively, leaders must pull them aside and describe what they've observed. They must show the gaps between observed values and desired values. And they must put values-misaligned players on a "values improvement plan." These players must embrace the values and behaviors within a short and specific time frame—or they must be lovingly set free.

The bottom line is that leaders must proactively reinforce values alignment, and they must not tolerate values misalignment. Going back to the performance-values matrix in Chapter 1, leaders want 99 percent of their players to be in the upper right quadrant: high performers *and* values alignment.

(Okay, you'd actually want 100 percent of players there, but I'm cutting you some slack. This requires constant effort!)

We'll discuss ways to deal with resistance to values alignment in Chapter 8.

Is it Responsibility or Accountability?

I've been very clear that gathering values data—the perceptions of whether or not leaders model stated department values and behaviors—is an accountability technique.

And some of you may believe that accountability is not the issue. I received a blog comment a few months ago chastising me about my thoughts on accountability. The commenter believes, "Leadership should not be about accountability! Authentic leadership is about responsibility!"

I believe that responsibility and accountability are different concepts—different in theory and in practice.

And both responsibility and accountability help ensure that performance promises *and* values promises are kept.

I believe that, when looking at performance expectations and values standards, responsibility is personal. I think that responsibility lies with individuals—individual leaders and individual team members.

In high-performing, values-aligned organizations, responsible individuals consistently apply their skills and commitment to deliver agreed-to goals and tasks on time, on budget, and exceeding quality requirements. In these organizations, individuals also embrace their responsibility to meet goal standards while demonstrating their company's espoused values.

In many of our organizations, though, performance expectations are not consistently met by every individual, be they leader or team member.

There might be many contributing factors to missed performance standards—overwhelming workload, poor skills for new expectations, lousy systems, competing priorities, team conflicts, lousy bosses, and so on. Any of these can erode one's ability to meet performance standards.

In many of our organizations, values expectations are not formalized. There are no explicit values expectations in your work environment—it's the Wild West. The only things that are measured, monitored, and rewarded are results.

That encourages players to get the results any way they can.

Have you ever attended a company awards banquet, and the highest "quota buster" salesperson is asked to come to the podium to accept his or her award? And it takes that person a while to make his or her way to the podium because of all the body bags the person is dragging?

That's a "win at all costs, no values to worry about here" work environment. We've all seen these environments.

In organizations that *do* have formalized values and behaviors, sometimes those values standards are not consistently met by every individual, be they leader or team member. That may happen more often than sometimes.

If values and behaviors are formalized but not reinforced—there's no values accountability—players will do what they've always done: Get the results in any way possible.

The fact remains that in some organizations—high-performing, values-aligned organizations—many more performance commitments are *made* than *missed*. Despite experiencing some of the same conditions and temptations that trip up lesser organizations, those best practice teams and companies consistently meet performance expectations *and* values standards—every day.

Is this success entirely driven by personal responsibility? Certainly individual responsibility does contribute—but it's not the only factor that drives consistent success.

I believe that organizational accountability closes any gaps that occur when individual responsibility falls short of agreed-to performance and values standards.

I believe that leaders are responsible for clarifying their team's purpose, values, strategy, and goals. They are, therefore, responsible for ensuring that every commitment made—for performance and for values—is met, day in and day out.

The only way leaders can ensure that promises are kept is to follow up and check in with team members regularly to see if progress is on track and to see if the organization's values and behaviors are being demonstrated by each team member.

If progress is being made according to plan and according to the team's values and behaviors, the leader can praise and encourage, and move on to another topic—or move on to conversations with another team member.

If, however, progress is not on track or if values are not consistently demonstrated, the leader must be consistent in monitoring activity, addressing gaps, and coaching team members back to standard.

If personal responsibility doesn't deliver promised results using the organization's values and behaviors, the leader must engage in accountability discussions to get folks back on track.

I hope I've made a strong case that personal responsibility and organizational accountability, together, ensure consistent performance and exceptional citizenship.

CRAFTING YOUR CUSTOM VALUES SURVEY

I've suggested that leaders use a variety of channels to learn the extent to which they are seen as modeling the department's values and behaviors. One of the most important tools for gauging values alignment is a custom values survey, taken by all leaders and employees in the organization every six months.

Most companies monitor performance metrics carefully to ensure that promised goals are delivered upon. These performance dashboards are a primary foundation of performance reviews. What the custom values survey does is add a values dashboard to the mix. It offers reliable, valid data about values alignment.

Performance dashboards are monitored daily. Valued behaviors need to be monitored daily, but a formal custom values survey needs to happen every six months.

Look at your custom values survey as a vital dashboard that requires monitoring and attending. You want formal data from this survey twice a year—not once in a blue moon, or once and never again.

When you start the values survey process, you make a commitment to continue the values survey process, twice a year, ad nauseam (forever).

Conducting a custom values survey makes values alignment as important as goal accomplishment. That's what is required to shift your organization into the upper right quadrant on the performance-values matrix: high performance *and* values alignment.

The survey questions are derived from the valued behaviors already formalized in your organizational constitution. These valued behaviors are easily translated into questions for the values survey.

Just as your valued behaviors are stated in desirable terms (describing how great citizens behave in the organization, not how lousy citizens behave), the items or questions in your custom values survey are stated in desirable terms.

I call this a "custom" values survey because no other company on the planet will have the exact same valued behaviors as your team, department, or company has. Your valued behaviors are unique. *You formally defined these specific behaviors because you know that's exactly how you want leaders and team members to behave.*

A generic survey won't give you the kind of actionable information you require on values alignment. You've already spent valuable time identifying desirable values and behaviors. I'll help you craft a custom values survey that will give you solid, undeniable information about which of your leaders is a model citizen—and which leaves much to be desired, citizenship-wise!

The great news is that the foundations of your custom values survey are already defined in the form of your valued behaviors. Ninety percent of your work is done! We'll build on these behaviors to create your custom values survey.

Let's examine how to build a survey item from a valued behavior.

We'll use one of the valued behaviors in my retail client's customer service value referred to earlier. The valued behavior states, "I initiate friendly hospitality by promptly and enthusiastically smiling and acknowledging everyone who comes within 10 feet."

That behavior would translate into a survey question that states:

My direct boss initiates friendly hospitality with me by promptly and enthusiastically smiling and acknowledging me when I come within 10 feet of him or her.

In the survey, items are rated using a six-point scale, as follows:

1—strongly disagree

2—disagree

3—slightly disagree

4—slightly agree

5—agree

6—strongly agree

We use an even-numbered scale so respondents *cannot select the middle ground*. If you use a five-point scale and respondents select "3" often, is that actionable data for you? Is "3" a good score or a not so good score?

You don't want to find yourself in the position of having to guess if that midpoint is good or bad. Use an even-numbered scale to eliminate the midpoint ranking.

I prefer a six-point scale to a four-point scale because it gives employees a wider range of response possibilities. And my clients and I have found that the six-point scale shown is easy for respondents to score and offers actionable data from the results.

Look at the rating scale as providing degrees of "yes, these valued behaviors are happening" and "no, these valued behaviors are not happening." Responses of 1 through 3 are degrees of no; responses of 4 through 6 are degrees of yes.

On this scale, what are good scores? You want high yes responses. Since all of the items or questions are stated in desirable terms, we want high numbers—5 or 6 on our six-point scale.

These scores mean that employees consistently agree or strongly agree that their leaders model the stated valued behaviors day in and day out.

The client example presents a challenge, though. There are two separate ideas in this behavioral statement. Take a look and see if you can identify them.

My direct boss initiates friendly hospitality with me by promptly and enthusiastically smiling and acknowledging me when I come within 10 feet of him or her.

Survey creators call this kind of item "two-tailed," meaning that it is asking two separate things in one question.

The first idea or behavior that the client wants to measure is "smiling" (promptly and enthusiastically, of course). The second idea or behavior the client wants to measure is "acknowledging me."

If a team member's boss demonstrates both these desired behaviors, all the time, promptly and enthusiastically *and* within 10 feet, answering this question won't pose any difficulties for team members.

However, what if a team member believes that the boss *smiles* promptly and enthusiastically but doesn't consistently *acknowledge* the team member?

If your questions are two-tailed, respondents may be confused about what you're asking. They may skip the question or give you unreliable responses, just to put a score down and move on to the next item.

Let's look at another potential problem with survey items. Here is an example from a different client's values survey:

I am comfortable being honest with my supervisor.

The problem with this question is that it is asking about comfort, not about behavior. A team member could respond with a 5 or 6 on our six-point scale, meaning the person is comfortable being honest. Does the response mean that the person actually *is* honest with the supervisor?

I don't think you care whether the team member is comfortable. I think you care about the team member actually *being honest*—having difficult conversations, disagreeing with a suggestion the boss makes, and so on.

The difference is subtle but incredibly important. Don't ask questions about what people think or what their attitude is. Ask questions about what people *do*, about their behavior and their leader's behavior.

I would rewrite this question so it's behavioral:

I express my honest opinions with my supervisor regularly.

This item now rates an observable behavior. Team members can more easily rank their agreement with this statement on our six-point scale.

Ensure that your custom values survey items present behaviors for rating, and you'll get reliable, actionable values data.

Depending on the number of valued behaviors in your organizational constitution, there could be 30 to 50 questions in the custom values survey. Answering 50 questions doesn't take long in this type of survey, typically less than 15 minutes.

I've had some clients who wanted their surveys to be no longer than 20 questions. A couple of others wanted to ask questions about valued behaviors in two or three different ways. They posed values questions about their organization (as a whole), separate values questions about the respondents' bosses, and separate values questions about their senior leadership team. They ended up with more than 100 questions on their surveys.

They got great, reliable, actionable data. Let's look at some of their questions and scores.

In the first section, rating their company as a whole, they posed questions like these:

"The culture at our company fosters mutual respect." (On a six-point scale, the average score for this item was 4.15.)

"Work discussions in our company focus on problems and processes, not people." (3.88 average)

"Efficiency and effectiveness are criteria used to evaluate work in our company." (4.15 average)

These scores fall below our 5- to 6-point target. There was clearly opportunity here to have desired valued behaviors demonstrated across different functions and teams in the company.

In the second section team members rated their direct supervisor. The client posed questions like these:

"My supervisor treats me with respect." (5.38 average)

"My supervisor keeps the commitments he or she has made to me." (5.32 average)

"I enjoy working for my supervisor." (5.42 average)

"My supervisor cooperates with other supervisors to meet company goals." (5.22 average)

"My supervisor supports the decisions I make in my area of responsibility." (5.26 average)

These scores are terrific, well within our desired target range. It is clear from these scores that team members trust and respect their supervisors. They see their bosses demonstrating the desired company-valued behaviors.

In the third section team members rated the executive team of the company. The client posed questions like:

"Executive team members make and keep their commitments." (4.28 average)

"Executive team members treat each other with respect." (4.39 average)

"The executive team demonstrates honesty and integrity." (4.32 average)

"The executive team shares information." (3.76 average)

These scores are below our desired target range of 5 to 6. The executive team scores were higher than the scores that the overall company earned, but not by much. There were certainly opportunities for the executive team to align more consistently with desired valued behaviors.

This is great data. It is actionable in that it shows where desired valued behaviors are not being seen by team members (in the company as a whole and with the executive team) and where those desired valued behaviors are being seen (with their supervisors).

However, you may not want a survey of 100 or more questions.

I suggest getting a core baseline on your valued behaviors with one question per behavior and no more than 10 department-wide

questions. That will keep the total number of questions to a manage-
able limit (30 to 50).

Remember that you're going to use this values survey data as a
baseline for assessing leaders' demonstration of valued behaviors *over
time*. You want to have the questions remain the same for the first two
runs of your survey, at which time you can make refinements to the
questions where needed.

This will give you reliable values data that you can compare across
multiple runs of your survey, year in and year out.

In the preceding chapter, we looked at some of the WD-40
Company's 2014 employee opinion survey results. The five top-scoring
items were rated at between 97.1 and 99.7 percent favorable. That's
outstanding alignment to the company's desired values and behaviors!

With our recommended six-point scale, we're looking for scores
of 5 or 6 (ratings of "agree" and "strongly agree") on every survey
item. A 5 on our six-point scale converts to 83 percent favorable; a
6 converts to 100 percent favorable. The five top-scoring items from
WD-40 Company's survey show that employees see desired values and
behaviors in action daily.

The client with more than 100 questions conducted its custom
values survey annually. This allowed it to gauge progress over time on
its values and valued behaviors. Here are the comparisons of the average
scores over two years across the client's three contexts (company,
supervisor, and executive team):

	Company	Supervisor	Executive Team
Year 1	4.39	5.20	4.42
Year 2	4.45	5.31	4.34

The benefit of the keeping same items in your survey over time
ensures the valid comparison across different runs of the values survey.

That's certainly the case for this client. These scores show that the
client made progress in the company-wide and supervisor contexts, but

lost ground in the executive team context. This is consistent with many clients' experiences in this organizational constitution process. As team members get smarter about what values alignment looks like, their expectations go up—particularly for leaders championing the culture refinement.

I've also seen this happen with team members' ratings of their boss from the first survey to the second survey. When team members are initially given the chance to rate their leader's values alignment, they're usually pretty nice. They give scores that are on the agreement side of the rankings.

However, some team members go the other direction in their responses to the first values survey. They've been keeping score in their heads and hearts for *decades* and now they've *finally* been given the chance to state their opinions. They zap their boss, giving very low scores.

They may not actually be disengaged—they've just never been given the chance to provide feedback before. So, they scour their scoreboard and rate their boss from the perspective of long-ago issues.

These zappers are usually the minority. Their votes count just the same as the nice votes—and there is usually a greater frequency of the nice votes.

Does that mean that the first run of the survey doesn't provide reliable information? It *is* providing reliable information! It's a snapshot point in time that needs to be taken seriously.

And, over time, team members' newness with the survey opportunity won't impact scores terribly much. You'll see scores stabilize after the third run and beyond. This is the "truth over time" scenario of team members' perceptions that you're looking for.

Here's another dynamic to consider. How will you administer your custom values survey? There are a number of online solutions that let respondents complete the survey on a computer, tablet, or smartphone. I'm a big fan of FluidSurveys.[1] One client used Cvent[2] for its custom values survey, which gathered data from more than 80,000 employees in a one-month time frame.

Your work environment may not be conducive to team members using technology to enter their survey responses. Old-fashioned paper and pencil will work—but it will require someone to enter responses into a database or spreadsheet for analysis and reporting. That extra step is an opportunity for data entry errors—but it'll work.

One client wanted to use computers for team members' responses but, 15 years ago in a blue-collar plant, not very many team members had computers at home. So, the client set up kiosks—PCs in enclosed cabinets, placed around the plant, available to anyone at any time. This worked well; the response rate was in the low 90 percent range, which is very good.

In addition, those kiosks were used to communicate performance data—how different shifts were delivering to desired metrics, when the next all-company meeting would be held, key announcements for all staff, and so on. The kiosks became a huge contributor to better communication, and were, of course, available for the next run of the custom values survey six months after the initial run.

LEADERS MUST BE RATED ON THEIR VALUES ALIGNMENT *FIRST*

Before any team members can be asked to embrace the new values and behaviors, leaders—those with formal supervisory responsibility—must put themselves on the line by living the values and behaviors and inviting feedback through the values survey.

Credibility for the liberating rules of your values and behaviors grows every time a leader models those values and behaviors. Credibility for your values and behaviors erodes quickly if team members don't see leaders as values role models in every interaction.

During the first run of the survey, only leaders will be rated on their values alignment. This first run of the survey should occur about six months after publication of your organizational constitution. This time frame gives leaders plenty of time to actively model desired values and behaviors—or to not actively model them.

It won't be until the second run of the survey that you will invite team members not only to rate their leaders but to rate their peers and themselves on their demonstration of your valued behaviors.

At this stage, we focus on the leaders of the department and their first custom values survey.

We discussed four possible reactions to values expectations and values accountability earlier in this chapter. Those reactions are (1) fully embracing the values and behaviors, (2) "wait and see"—waiting to see if this is something those leaders really have to model, (3) self-selecting out of the organization (leaving), or (4) "stay and resist"—defying the values demands from within the organization.

If any leaders have self-selected out, we don't have to worry about them anymore. They're not going to engage in the custom values survey.

The other three reaction types *will* engage in the custom values survey—ready or not!

The ratings that team members give their leaders—and that leaders will see in their values profiles—will very likely show that team members observe and understand their bosses' degree of values alignment every day, high or low.

In other words, there are *logical consequences* to a leader's degree of values alignment. For leaders who have chosen to embrace the valued behaviors, their team members see it—and rank what they see in the survey. These leaders' values profiles should reflect their active values demonstration. For leaders who have chosen to *not* embrace the valued behaviors (the "wait and see" or "stay and resist" groups), their values profiles should reflect their *lack* of values demonstration.

Logical consequences are another term for the concept of perfection! It is what it is. Each leader's values profile should reflect what team members observe of their boss's valued behaviors over time.

Some of the items in your custom values survey may ask for values data from outside the team members' intact team and boss. Just as with the client example earlier in this chapter, you might ask company-wide or executive team questions in addition to questions regarding leaders' values alignment.

The company-wide and executive team questions will provide you with relevant data—but not the most critical data.

The most important data points in your custom values survey are team members' perceptions of their bosses—team members' beliefs on the degree to which their bosses live your valued behaviors. Each leader's profile is the most relevant metric for values alignment across your team or department!

Once you close the window on survey submissions, it'll take a few weeks to tally responses, analyze the data, and create the profiles for your contexts: a company-wide profile, an executive team profile, and a profile for every formal leader, manager, and supervisor in your department.

You'll distribute the company and executive team data to every player in the department. You'll debrief your key insights in an all-hands session, celebrating top scores and reviewing low scores. You probably won't have plans to address gaps outlined quite yet, but you'll let everyone know that you'll announce those various approaches in the weeks to come.

And you'll actually make plans and share them, in days—not weeks. You owe it to leaders and team members to respond to their survey input promptly. Don't mask any bad news (like the client I reported on a few chapters ago). Get it out. Make your plans. Announce your plans. Implement your plans.

Be sure to celebrate the top scores where you are seen as values aligned.

At the same time as your all-hands session, you'll give leaders their personal values profiles. Their profiles will include their self-perceptions as well as those of their direct reports (team members they formally supervise).

Every leader will fall somewhere between highly values aligned (scoring "strongly agree" or "agree" from their team members) and not particularly values aligned (scoring from "slightly agree" to "strongly disagree").

Every leader will have some things to celebrate (some will have more to celebrate than others!). Every leader will have valued behaviors to improve on.

Every leader needs to receive one-on-one coaching soon after receiving his or her values profile. With their boss, leaders must analyze their personal profiles and (1) celebrate alignment seen by team members, and (2) create a plan for addressing gaps and improving their values alignment as seen by team members.

Note that leaders' leaders who need to do values coaching may not possess demonstrated skills at values coaching today! That may be a skill gap you need to address before you conduct the first run of your custom values survey.

Within days, all leaders will need to debrief their personal values profiles with their intact teams. They must share the good news (high values scores) and the not so good news (low values scores). They need to outline their plan for being intentional with valued behaviors—and to demonstrate valued behaviors more frequently.

They need to ask team members for their help—by requesting them to provide regular feedback when they see either terrific values alignment or not so good values alignment.

Then, those leaders need to work their values plan, engage with team members, and learn from team members daily.

It's at this stage that those "wait and see" leaders will need to engage fully in values alignment. They won't be able to stay on the sidelines anymore, not with team member scores staring them in the face in the form of their values profiles.

They may choose to engage and embrace your valued behaviors—or they may choose to resist embracing your valued behaviors. It's their choice. Once they choose, you can celebrate their alignment, or lovingly set them free if they choose to ignore your valued behaviors.

It's also at this stage that your "stay and resist" players must choose—to engage and embrace, or to stay and resist more. It's their choice, and you'll respond appropriately to their choices.

Some of these players may self-select out when they see that their values profiles show how poorly aligned they are with the department's values and behaviors.

That's okay. If they're not going to be able to evolve into high-performing leaders who embrace your values, you can't keep them in your new culture.

There's one more thing to consider—the response rate to your survey.

A good response rate to your first custom values survey run is 70 to 80 percent; 81 percent or higher would be a terrific response rate. Less than 70 percent is not good.

What impacts the response rate? First is team members' belief that their responses will be *confidential*—no one will be able to attribute their responses to them.

As we've noted, team members have never been asked to provide values feedback before. Some may be fearful of providing honest opinions, so they'll choose not to take the survey. Some of those folks will take the survey, but they won't be as critical of the department, executives, or their boss as they want to be.

You need to be honest with team members. Their data will be rolled up into the broader company or department data and the executive team data, so there's little chance of anyone knowing who rated what high or low.

In their team leader's profile, though, their responses will be included with their teammates' responses in their boss's scores. In a team of 10 players, that's not too risky. In a team of three players, that can feel a bit riskier.

In a team of two, that feels extremely risky.

So, if a leader has less than three respondents' data available, don't run a profile for him or her. The risk of identifying responses is too great; the confidentiality of team members' responses is at risk, as well.

Let team members know that leader values profiles won't be run if there are fewer than three respondents. That will increase team members' trust that their answers will remain confidential.

The second thing that impacts response rate is that you engage with players *promptly* after the values survey. You tell them what you learned—the good and the bad. You share your plans quickly to address gaps identified in the values survey. And you put your plans into action quickly.

Prompt, consistent plans, decisions, and actions that address values gaps will make a huge difference. *Action* will boost team members' confidence that you are serious about crafting a values-aligned workplace.

Doing these two things will help your response rate immensely. Who knows? You might enjoy the 98 percent response rate that the WD-40 Company enjoyed in its 2014 employee opinion survey.

The next chapter presents proven practices for dealing with resistance to your organizational constitution.

CHAPTER 8

Dealing with Resistance

An organizational constitution changes expectations of leaders in your team or department significantly. Most leaders have never been held accountable to a constitution or to values standards. Some will demonstrate resistance in various forms: passivity, aggression, or that delightful combination of passive-aggressiveness.

The primary champion of the organizational constitution is the leader of that team or department. It is incumbent on that champion to address any resistance with a kind yet firm hand. The consistent message must be, "This train has left the station. This is what we're going to do. This is what we're going to be. Get on board—or get off the train."

To a great extent, the creation of an organizational constitution redefines the job of a great leader. A great job is not about managing processes and results—it's about *managing people's energy*. It's not about creating stakeholder value at any cost (human, reputation, etc.)—it's about creating a safe, inspiring workplace where employees invest their discretionary energy in solving problems and wowing customers.

This chapter presents ways that leaders can proactively address the resistance that some players in your team, department, or company will demonstrate when you engage them in the organizational constitution transformation.

Leaders must be prepared to deal promptly with resistance from across the department. Push back about values, behaviors, and alignment will emerge from all levels: members of the executive team, leaders and managers, team leads, and even team members in your organization.

Let's look at where you stand right now with your organizational constitution. If you've been putting these pieces into place:

- You have "started with YOU." You've crafted your personal purpose, values, and behaviors. You've clarified who you are as a person and what inspires you. You've built a solid foundation upon which to effectively lead the implementation of an organizational constitution with your team or department or company.

- You've drafted your team or department's purpose, its reason for being. You've formalized *what* the team does, for *whom*, and *why* it's important.

- You've formalized the values you want *everyone* on your team or department to demonstrate in *every* interaction—with bosses, peers, and even customers. You've defined your values in observable, tangible, measurable terms in the form of valued behaviors. You've socialized those values and behaviors with leaders and team members across your department, so everyone understands how values alignment should look, sound, and feel.

- You've formalized your business strategic plan, describing opportunities and imperatives that will enable the business to grow and thrive. You've aligned specific goals for each strategic imperative so that progress on your strategic plan is easy to monitor.

- And, you've set up a system to gather data on leaders' values demonstration. Team members will complete a custom values survey twice a year, rating the degree to which their leaders demonstrate your stated values and behaviors.

Even if you've not yet built some of these pieces, you're still reading!

If you're still reading, you must be intrigued with the concept of an organizational constitution. You're learning the core elements. You understand how these elements enable top performance and great team member citizenship. We hope we can say you are on the cusp of putting elements of your organizational constitution into action.

You've already invested a lot of time and energy thinking about how to create a safe, inspiring work environment for your team, department, or company. You've decided how you'll build a culture of "upper righters" from the performance-values matrix—team members who exceed performance expectations while modeling your valued behaviors every minute.

Many of you have begun building your safe, inspiring work environment, sharing the elements of your organizational constitution with leaders and team members. You've cleared the way and turned on the klieg lights to highlight the path.

Why would you let people off the hook now?

Why would you allow people to thumb their noses at your organizational constitution?

Why would you let leaders ignore the department's carefully crafted values and behaviors—and just focus on results, like before?

If you do let some players off the hook and not demand that they embrace your organizational culture, what is the not-so-subtle message you're broadcasting?

The message is clear: "Our organizational constitution really doesn't matter. As you were! Go back to our old, performance-focused ways and bad behavior."

If you allow *one* values-misaligned leader or player to continue his or her bad behavior after you've implemented your organizational constitution, you've pulled the rug out from under your values-aligned players.

It's a promise made ("We're going to align to our values!") that is boldly unkept. Your word—what you commit to—is not trustworthy. Your credibility will take a huge hit.

I'd be surprised if anyone in your organization believed anything you said moving forward, ever again. At minimum, people will wait and see if you'll really stick to what you promise down the line.

That's not a desirable state. Once you head down the organizational constitution path, you can't stop and you can't backtrack.

Keeping your players aligned takes constant tending, coaching, modeling, and reinforcing.

Keeping your own plans, decisions, and actions aligned takes constant tending. Keeping your leaders' and team members' plans, decisions, and actions aligned takes constant tending as well.

You simply can't tolerate bad behavior from anyone.

This chapter's Culture Effectiveness Assessment gauges how well you proactively address resistance in your department today.

Culture Effectiveness Assessment #8: Addressing Resistance	Strongly Disagree	Disagree	Slightly Disagree	Slightly Agree	Agree	Strongly Agree
1. Misaligned Leaders Are Told When data and observation leads to leaders being seen as values misaligned, they are told that it's a problem and it must be fixed.	1	2	3	4	5	6
2. Misaligned Leaders Are Coached Misaligned leaders are assigned a mentor or coach whose job it is to engage, gain the leader's commitment, and guide traction to values alignment.	1	2	3	4	5	6
3. Misaligned Leaders Are Given a Chance These leaders may never have been asked to operate in a values-aligned environment. They are given a second chance, but maybe not a third.	1	2	3	4	5	6
4. Misaligned Leaders Are Observed Closely Misaligned leaders are carefully scrutinized for values alignment. Team members are involved in providing observations. More frequent surveying of values alignment is the norm.	1	2	3	4	5	6

Culture Effectiveness Assessment #8: Addressing Resistance	Strongly Disagree	Disagree	Slightly Disagree	Slightly Agree	Agree	Strongly Agree
5. **Failure to Align Means Being Set Free** If coaching, observation, and regular feedback don't align the leader's values, he or she is asked to leave the organization.	1	2	3	4	5	6

Do others in your department know who is not on board? Of course they do. They see these resistant leaders' (and team members') misaligned behaviors every day.

Other leaders and team members wonder, "Why do they let her (or him) get away with that behavior? She's not modeling our values, that's for sure!"

Who is the "they" these observers are referring to? You, the leader of the team or department. You need to prepare yourself for the time and energy required to nudge and coach folks who are off track to get back on track—or out of your organization.

Who are the leaders and team members who will resist the values alignment effort? If we go back to the four ways players will react to your organizational constitution, we know that the players who embrace your values aren't resisting. They're embracing your organizational constitution. We don't have to worry about them!

Another group of players who are not resisting are those who have already chosen to leave your team or department. They have self-selected out and are not a worry at this time.

That leaves the "wait and see" players and the "stay and resist" players. Both demonstrate resistance to your organizational constitution.

The "wait and see" leaders and team members are less likely to be verbal or combative. They stay under the radar, trying not to stand out as they watch passively to see if this shift will actually demand that they engage in it.

The "stay and resist" leaders and team members are more likely to be verbal or combative. They are bolder with their concerns and questions. Their concerns are typically driven by fear and concerns about power.

Some leaders will see the organizational constitution as eroding their long-established power structure. They won't appreciate their influence—their control—being messed with.

Some leaders will experience fear of the unknown. They don't know what is expected of them in this new world. What they've known is now changing, so they are concerned they may not have the skills to lead in that new world.

Their fear of the unknown is a powerful driver. They have never lived in a work environment that outlined great citizenship behaviors. The only work environments they know have operated by power, politics, and fear. These folks have no idea what their evolving work environment will look like—or whether they will be able to exist in that new environment, much less thrive in it.

This fear of the unknown raises another root cause—skill gaps. Leaders may not have demonstrated the skills required to model your valued behaviors. They may not have every demonstrated the skills to praise and encourage others.

They may not have ever demonstrated the skills at mentoring and coaching values alignment in others.

Skill gaps are reasonably easy to address. We know what behaviors result in consistent modeling of values, consistent reinforcement of values, and consistent coaching for values alignment. We can teach those!

What may stand in the way of skill building is the resistant leaders' lack of willingness to *learn* and lack of willingness to *adopt* these new behaviors.

Ultimately, you have to address their willingness first. If your coaching helps them be open to learning and adopting, you can engage in teaching and observing their adoption of the new valued behaviors.

It does little good to begin teaching if your resistant leaders don't see the benefit of leading from a values base *and* a performance base. It's like teaching a pig to sing—the effort is exhausting for both parties, and the result isn't good for anyone.

It's important to note that these leaders probably won't *say* they have these fears, but that's what is likely at the root of their discontent.

Here's your charge. Once you engage your team or department on the organizational constitution journey and you demonstrate the valued behaviors and inspire others to demonstrate them, you must be vigilant for early adopters and "suspect components" along the way.

You must be on the lookout for early adopters and proactive champions of your desired values and behaviors. Recognizing and celebrating these players will boost confidence in the change and create momentum for the change.

Praising values-aligned behavior helps encourage greater frequency of those valued behaviors in others—the player you praise and the players who observe you praising.

You must be on the lookout for any suspect components, as well. I learned of the "suspect component" concept while reading Marcus Luttrell's book, *Lone Survivor*.[1] In it, Marcus describes how U.S. Navy SEAL boot camp was a ruthless elimination process for an elite fighting force that "cannot tolerate a suspect component." The incredible physical and mental demands on SEAL candidates ensured that only the strongest made it through.

Suspect components are leaders who do not embrace your organizational constitution, nor do they lead the charge to encourage others to embrace your organizational constitution. Suspect components are weak links in your leadership chain.

If suspect components are allowed to remain in place, it's only a matter of time before they fail. In your organization, their failure may erode belief in and momentum of your desired high-performing, values-aligned work environment.

WHAT DOES RESISTANCE LOOK LIKE?

Leaders, managers, and supervisors will be the source of the initial resistance. That's not surprising, since you're asking these formal leaders to embrace the new values and behaviors first. Later, some team members may express resistance—but fewer will do so if you've got a united front of leaders who have embraced the organizational constitution.

Resistance can be expressed in many forms. Leaders who in the past have been calm and cool may demonstrate frustration and anger. Leaders who in the past have said the right things but done their own thing might be much more likely to act out in meetings, not just behind closed doors.

Some resistance activities are very obvious and visible—they are acts of rebellion. Other resistance activities are more nuanced and much harder to see. These subtle expressions can be immensely powerful, eroding team members' confidence in the organizational constitution initiative, in the leaders promoting values alignment, and even in their own place in the evolving work environment.

The most common categories of leaders' resistance to the values alignment process are the following:

- **Don't walk the walk.** These leaders typically say the right things in meetings but don't model the valued behaviors in day-to-day interactions. They ignore the new practices and keep doing what they've always been doing.

  These leaders are not typically open to feedback about others' perceptions of their values alignment. They close off those discussions before they get too deep. Or, they might listen and nod their heads, and promise to do better. But their plans, decisions, and actions do not support the new organizational constitution.

- **Undermine the initiative.** These leaders discount the organizational constitution and values alignment. They not only don't model the values, but they also tease others about them. They roll their eyes at the mention of values alignment. They complain often that the initiative is a waste of time.

They may be calm and professional when they erode your organizational constitution or they may be bold and angry. Either way, they are consistent in their efforts to derail the values alignment process, quickly and thoroughly.

There are numerous other ways that leaders resist change, but most resistance behaviors fall logically into these two categories.

You can easily see that these resistant leaders do not reside in the upper-right quadrant of the performance-values matrix. They're on the left side of that model because they're not demonstrating your valued behaviors. Depending on their performance to standards, they are either upper-lefters (high performance but low values match) or lower-lefters (low performance and low values match).

Leaders and team members in those quadrants aren't going to be fun to work with, nor will they advance the culture to align with your organizational constitution.

How do most leaders react to resistance to policies or procedures in their work environment?

Most leaders *do nothing*. They resist dealing with others' resistance!

Why? Many leaders are uncomfortable engaging others in accountability conversations. Disagreements can occur. Conflict can occur. Despite the huge negative impact of players ignoring the values standards in place, leaders resist engaging in these conversations.

Many leaders simply *hope* the resistance just goes away. They might think, "If I ignore them, they'll get tired of complaining and get on board. It'll just take a few weeks."

(Hope is not a sustainable strategy!)

Have you ever seen resistance to a new policy simply disappear? That doesn't happen very often. Usually the resistance continues, for weeks and months.

HOW MUST A LEADER ADDRESS RESISTANCE?

Unfortunately, there is not a values-alignment pill on the market. I keep telling my pharmaceutical clients that there's a gold mine out there if they could craft such a pill! No such luck at this point in time.

The following approach works very well. It is a direct, firm, and encouraging approach. It aligns perfectly with the "define the way," "model the way," and "align the way" phases of implementing your organizational constitution.

First, don't take the resistance personally. These players don't have it in for you; they just don't want to go where you're asking them to go. The resistance is not about *you*—it's about *them*.

If you're upset with the resisters, I don't blame you. However, you won't be able to facilitate this discussion effectively if you're amped up. I suggest you defer the conversation for a few hours until you're in a calm, coaching state of mind.

Second, your job is to present what you've heard and observed in a calm, nonblaming, nonjudgmental manner. You're presenting factual information. You've seen their misaligned behavior, you've received feedback from others about their misaligned behavior, and you're presenting those observations in a factual manner.

Don't focus on their attitudes or beliefs—that's a difficult row to hoe. Their motivations are certainly interesting, but motivations are not relevant. In essence, you don't care what they believe! Their observable, tangible, measurable behaviors are relevant—and it's those resistant behaviors you want to change.

You need to present the information on the person's behavior so that the listener—the resisting leader—can understand that the behavior has been noticed and it needs to change.

Third, you need to understand the resister's perspective. You can listen without agreeing with everything someone says. Give the resisting leaders a forum for expressing their concerns and fears about this change. Reflect on what you've learned from them, helping them feel heard.

Fourth, you can't budge—every leader must be fully on board, fully and consistently in the upper-right quadrant of the performance-values matrix. You can communicate to them that the rules have changed. You can explain how there's a new standard in place, for both performance and values—and that all leaders must be credible role models.

You need to tell them that you won't let them off the hook. *Values alignment is nonnegotiable.*

You must express, clearly and succinctly, that you expect values alignment from all department leaders and team members. There's no "kind of" values alignment space in which to hang out in your department. People either demonstrate values alignment or they don't.

(Just like there isn't a "kind of pregnant" space. Either you are or you're not!)

Finally, your job is to give the resistant leaders a chance to align to your organizational constitution. If they agree to embrace your valued behaviors, map out a plan for them. Be specific about the behaviors you expect. Be specific about the behaviors you will not tolerate. Gain their agreement on the values standards. And explain what will happen if they do embrace your organizational constitution (continued meaningful employment), and explain what will happen if they are unable to model the valued behaviors.

You will basically serve as a values accountability coach for the resistant leader.

The logical consequence of resisting leaders' failure to embrace your organizational constitution is that they must be lovingly set free. They will have to find somewhere else to work, since they're unable to deliver the values expectations *and* performance expectations that you now demand.

What if they don't agree to your plan? What if they don't see values alignment as important—and they choose to ignore your organizational constitution? If they choose to ignore your values and behaviors, they're not willing partners of yours in this culture refinement.

If they can't fit in, you must help them out—out of the organization. You'll do so kindly yet firmly. You'll say, "This is no longer a good
fit for you or for us. Let's work together to transition you out of the team
as quickly and smoothly as possible."

You won't *judge* their choices, and you won't *budge* on your
demands for values alignment.

What if they threaten to quit? That is a bullying tactic—and it
doesn't serve that leader well. Bullying isn't likely to be found on your
list of valued behaviors, is it?

If they threaten to quit, you might calmly and firmly say, "That's
certainly an option. If you are unable to embrace our values and
behaviors, that might be the best way for you to go."

Your desire as you engage with resistant leaders is to help them
see the benefit of coming on board. You'd rather they embrace your
organizational constitution than defy it. And, if they choose to ignore
your values and behaviors, separation is a likely outcome—sooner
or later.

Be sure to engage your human resources experts as early as possible
to ensure you are lawful and fair in processing any leader's or team
member's separation from the organization.

How many chances should resistant leaders get? Is it fair to give
resistant leaders the opportunity to learn that you are serious about
values alignment—and to give them a second chance? I think that's fair.
After all, you've really changed up the expectations for leaders, and they
may need some prodding and coaching to embrace the new rules.

Give them a second chance, and observe them carefully. If you
don't see sincere effort and progress toward values alignment, you need
to call them on it, and proceed with their transition out of the
organization.

If you *do* see sincere effort and progress toward values alignment,
celebrate it and continue praising and observing. You might find that
the previously resistant leader has become one of the biggest supporters
of your organizational constitution.

I'm not a big believer in third chances. If resistant leaders haven't changed the color of their stripes through a second chance, it's unlikely they'll do so with yet another chance.

Make the call. Lovingly set them free. It would be better to have someone in the role who embraces the values and can learn the skills (a lower-righter in the performance-values matrix) than to have someone who actively denigrates your values and behaviors.

What if you can't set them free? What if their employment scenario doesn't allow for them to be fired? Some of my clients face this situation. They've found two avenues that might help reduce the negative impact of values-misaligned players.

First, insulate these players from as many interactions with others as possible. Find them a role and an office where they don't engage with internal team members or external customers, ever. At least minimize the people who must interact with these players.

Second, don't back down on the values demands. Let them keep their role, interacting with whomever their role requires. Observe their every plan, decision, and action. Closely scrutinize their behavior. Coach them often. Praise aligned behavior and redirect misaligned behavior.

Don't let them off the hook.

It'll take time and energy on your part and others' parts. Make it clear that values alignment is the path you want them on.

They'll tire of the constant scrutiny and coaching. They'll either align or self-select out.

These are challenging scenarios for you to deal with. It's not fun to deal with unhappy and assertive (or aggressive) leaders or team members. Yet you must address the resistance and rid your team, department, or company of values-misaligned players.

Your goal is to have 100 percent of your leaders and team members in the upper-right quadrant—high performers who are great team citizens.

That'll take some tending, maintenance, and trimming.

CHAPTER 9

Hiring for Values Alignment

A t this stage, if you've been putting the pieces of your organizational constitution in place in your department, you're seeing the benefits. Our clients typically enjoy greater workplace inspiration within six months of embedding the purpose, values, and behaviors embodied in an organizational constitution.

Players in your department—leaders and team members—enjoy better relationships, better performance, and better customer experiences. Proactive problem solving begins to happen more frequently.

Players start feeling the power of working with team members who have shared goals and common values.

At this stage, however, you may not have all players 100 percent aligned. You may be dealing with pockets of resistance or periodic exclamations of "This is harder than I thought" from leaders and team members. You may feel like it's two steps forward and one step back. You're making progress but you wish it were faster.

But you've got a critical mass going. It is hoped that you're seeing leaders and team members approaching the tipping point where there is significantly greater confidence in the organizational constitution and the direction the culture is going.

Take a breath and enjoy it, for a moment.

There.

Now, it is time to discuss proven ways to integrate new leaders and team members into your evolving department culture.

You put your desired culture at risk every time you hire someone. You put your culture at even greater risk every time you hire a leader, someone who will have formal responsibility for guiding the work of others.

If that leader doesn't embrace your organizational culture, he or she will erode trust, respect, and workplace safety. Hiring a values-misaligned leader or team member will be another not-so-subtle message: "That constitution thing? A little joke! We're not really going to manage to those values!"

We'll look at the best practices for hiring values-aligned players and orienting values-aligned players. You won't enjoy consistent performance and values alignment from new hires if you're not extremely intentional about both hiring and orientation.

This chapter's Culture Effectiveness Assessment allows you to rate your hiring and orientation practices today.

Culture Effectiveness Assessment #9: Aligned Hiring	Strongly Disagree	Disagree	Slightly Disagree	Slightly Agree	Agree	Strongly Agree
1. Values Are Shared with Candidates Recruitment for any role emphasizes our team's unique culture and the requirement for all players to demonstrate our valued behaviors.	1	2	3	4	5	6
2. Interview Questions Focus on Values More than half of the interview engages candidates in discussions about our team's values in action, quandaries they might face, how they would address values conflicts, and so on.	1	2	3	4	5	6
3. Team Members Participate in Interviews A potential team member's interview process includes time with a cross-functional panel of current team members to have them gauge the candidate's culture fit.	1	2	3	4	5	6

Culture Effectiveness Assessment #9: Aligned Hiring	Strongly Disagree	Disagree	Slightly Disagree	Slightly Agree	Agree	Strongly Agree
4. Leaders Participate in Interviews A potential leader's interview process includes time with current department leaders to have them gauge the candidate's culture fit.	1	2	3	4	5	6
5. New Hire Orientation Emphasizes Values All new hires complete a thorough orientation to the department's organizational constitution, including an overview of our custom values survey, values alignment expectations, and so on.	1	2	3	4	5	6

HOW DO YOU HIRE TODAY?

The most important part of *how* you hire is *whom* you hire today. What is it that you look for in a candidate that tells you, "Yes, this person will fit in and help move us forward"?

If your team or company is like most others across the globe today, the primary lens you use when hiring new players is that of skills and past accomplishments. Applicable skills and past successes are great—but the talented player who doesn't embrace your department's values and behaviors will cause much grief (and take up much time and energy).

If you only pay attention to a candidate's skills and past performance but do not assess the candidate's ability to demonstrate your values and behaviors, you could be bringing in an "upper-lefter" on the performance-values matrix—a high performer with a low values match.

You can't be casual about hiring for the values match!

In a 2013 *Fast Company* interview,[1] Warby Parker co-CEO Neil Blumenthal said the small company's biggest lesson in 2012 was how to scale its unique culture.

Blumenthal described hiring a smart, capable player who worked hard and was nice to customers—but one of Warby Parker's valued behaviors was to be super-friendly. They coached this young man to get him to change his tone but he just couldn't adapt. They had to let him go.

Blumenthal and his co-CEO Dave Gilboa realized that as the company grew, they couldn't maintain the culture through strong individual relationships. So, they built a culture interview SWAT team that does 75 percent of the interviewing process.

Hootsuite CEO Ryan Holmes shared this insight in a 2013 blog post:[2] "One subpar employee can throw an entire department into disarray." The impact of a bad hire on productivity and team morale is huge.

You probably have your own stories to add. We've all made hiring mistakes and seen the short-term and long-term costs those decisions created.

Here's one more consideration before we dive into hiring and orientation practices. How do outsiders—members of the broader organization or of your community—perceive your department or plant? What's your team's buzz?

When you craft a high-performing, values-aligned team, the buzz is positive. People learn about your team or department from friends or family members who work there. People across the organization hear good things about your team's performance and your team's morale.

It may take some time, but that buzz will help attract candidates to you for consideration.

Here's an example. One culture client is three years into its transformation, and is doing great. Volume is up. Customer satisfaction is up. Employee engagement has never been higher.

Recently this client engaged in a job fair in its community. Company leaders told me they'd never seen such strong interest from people who want to work for them. The line of job seekers at their booth didn't slow down the entire afternoon. They even received resumes from a few people who were working other company booths at the fair!

That's a very good buzz. That good buzz has built up the client's resume pool very quickly. The company can now sift through these candidates and find values-aligned players who will fit its culture and contribute to its success.

BEFORE THE HIRE—RECRUITING, INTERVIEWING, AND ASSESSING

What is the condition of your team or company's brand in your industry and community? Do potential leaders and team members know what you produce and/or sell, but know little more?

If you only want to attract skilled candidates, that's the only messaging you need.

However, we know you don't want "just" skilled candidates—you want skilled candidates who will also enthusiastically embrace your team's purpose, values, behaviors, strategies, and goals.

You want skilled leaders and team members who understand what your company stands for, why you do what you do, and for whom. Your purpose statement can become the first filter for potential hires.

The second filter for candidates is your values list, which outlines the principles that guide every plan, decision, and action. You must educate potential leaders and team members about your values and behaviors.

Be intentional with your team or company's brand. Be intentional with your team or company's story—*why* you all do what you do, and to serve whom.

The better educated your candidate pool is about who you are, what you do, and what you stand for, the more likely you will attract values-aligned players who are very interested in working for your team.

Candidates scour the web these days for information about potential employers. Does your team or department have a web home? Does that web home serve as an attractive, educational place telling about what it's like to work on your team or in your department? Does it clearly define your team's purpose, values, and behaviors?

If it doesn't, refine it so it does.

Find websites that do a great job of describing the culture of that team or department. Two sites worth visiting and learning from are Warby Parker[3] and The Mission Continues.[4] Warby Parker is an eyewear designer and retailer that gives away a pair of eyeglasses to someone in need for every pair sold. To date, the company has distributed 500,000 free pairs of eyeglasses!

The Mission Continues is a nonprofit that provides U.S. military veterans with new missions after they return home. The organization deploys veterans in fellowship programs through partnership with nonprofit organizations in their communities and in service platoons where veterans work with local partners to build stronger communities.

Both of these organizations' websites do a terrific job of presenting the what, the why, and the how of their team (purpose, values, behaviors, and even strategies).

Make sure every job posting includes an explanation of your team purpose and values. If there is space, add details about your valued behaviors, and about the requirement for all leaders and team members to model these behaviors. If there is not space, add a link to your web home where candidates can find these details.

Ensure that your applications and your recruitment process meet all federal and state requirements. Conduct background checks and employment eligibility verifications as required.

And, don't stop there. Be sure to add questions that give candidates the opportunity to describe their own work ethic and their experiences with values in the workplace in past positions. Ask candidates why they want to work with your team or department. Ask candidates which one of your values excites them the most.

Then, review these answers carefully. Screen candidates' applications to bring in only those with the greatest potential to demonstrate your values and fit into your culture. Don't waste time interviewing applicants with great skill sets but who show little interest in your values and behaviors.

When you bring in candidates for their interviews, ensure that all required personnel forms and permissions are completed.

Make sure that at least half of the interview focuses on your team purpose, values, and behaviors. Ask questions that let candidates share how they would deal with values conflicts or ethical dilemmas—not just how they would use their technical skills to complete an activity.

Ensure that the candidate engages with current leaders and team members, one-on-one or in small group conversations, to enable both parties to ask questions about skills and culture requirements.

One CEO I've worked with engages in a bit of subterfuge when interviewing candidates for leadership roles in his company. Two of his company's values are "show backbone" and "show respect." He spends about an hour with leadership candidates. He arranges for his assistant to call his cell phone about 30 minutes into the interview. His phone rings, he says, "Excuse me for a moment," and he answers the call. He spends only a minute on the phone, then reengages with the candidate.

At the end of the interview, the CEO asks, "How could I have made this a better experience for you?" The candidates with backbone will say something like, "I wish you hadn't answered your phone call in the middle of my interview. That didn't feel very respectful."

That's what this CEO wants to see—a values-driven player who is unafraid to call out disrespectful behavior.

Candidates who do not show backbone to this CEO at that moment are unlikely to be hired.

It's an effective approach and clearly premeditated. Include situations that you want to test candidates on so you can see how they react. Values alignment may require that candidates question something they experienced in the interview!

Give the candidates time to ask any questions that they have about the job, team, or department. After all, you want them to interview *you* as much as you are interviewing *them*. Each candidate needs to be confident that he or she is coming to a team with a safe, inspiring work environment—and to a team that will help the candidate succeed and fit in well.

You'll assess the candidate for needed skills and required team citizenship at every phase—recruitment, application, and interview. If you are satisfied with both, you can proceed to an offer. If you are not satisfied with both, should you thank the candidate for his or her time and interest, say that it's not a good fit, and wish the person well?

Let's think this through for a moment.

What if the values fit is terrific but the candidate doesn't have demonstrated skills for the job at hand? This describes the "lower-righter" on the performance-values matrix. I suggested in Chapter 1 that the lower-righters who are already in your department deserve a chance. They need to boost their contribution through skill building or through a job change internally so they genuinely contribute.

What about the values-aligned candidates who may not have the skills you're hiring for right now? Do they deserve a chance?

Adding values-aligned players is always a good thing. It helps deepen the traction of your organizational constitution through greater understanding of purpose, valued behaviors, strategies, and goals, and through the alignment to those each day.

But you must gauge the risks of hiring someone into a role where the person doesn't yet have needed job skills. It will take time to build team member skills. You must assess whether the pressure to produce immediately can be adapted to allow for skill building.

If the production time frame can handle that delay, make a job offer. If the production time frame cannot be adapted, tell candidates why you cannot make an offer at this time. Tell them their values are a great match but their skills don't fit the role available.

And let them know you'll keep their resume and application on file for such time when a job role opens up that fits their skill sets or that will enable skill building over time.

What if you're hiring for a specific skill set? Some projects or solutions might require technical skills that are beyond the capability of your current team members. You might find a candidate with those skills but who is not a good culture fit; the person doesn't share the department's values and doesn't express an interest in your "values thing."

A number of culture clients have run into this issue, and it's solved by contracting for that skill set. You don't bring that player (or those players) into the organization—that wouldn't work on a number of fronts. You hire the needed skills on a contractor basis and insulate those players from your department.

They're hired on a contractor basis for specific skills. They apply those skills and deliver what you need from outside your organization. No harm done. Once their portion of the project is complete, their contract is ended.

The primary driver of your decision to hire or not—and how to leverage their values and/or skills—is their ability to fit into your culture, to model your valued behaviors.

I suggest that every candidate undergo a probationary period, a 90-day time frame where the candidate and the team can test out how good their skills match up and how good the culture fit is. Make the employment offer a probationary one.

If both candidate and team are pleased at the end of 90 days, a permanent offer can be extended.

If after the probationary period one party or the other is *not* satisfied with the skills match or the culture fit, thank the candidate for his or her time. Tell such candidates it's not a good fit, wish them well, and release them from their probationary contract.

AFTER THE HIRE—ORIENTATION AND INTEGRATION

How much time does your team or company spend today on orienting new hires?

My informal research indicates that new team members complete a two-day orientation (on average). New leaders complete a four- or five-day orientation (on average).

What is the most effective time duration to orient new leaders or team members? It depends. It should take as much time as the candidate needs—which will likely be two or three weeks, or even longer.

The amount of time, alone, isn't an indication of a high-quality orientation. What's important is what is involved in your orientation: the activities, support, and ongoing guidance new hires receive to help them succeed in their roles.

All of us have stories of really lousy orientation practices over our careers.

One salesperson told me that her orientation was two hours long on the first morning in her new job. All the personnel and benefits forms were completed, the harassment policy and other guidelines were explained and duly signed, and she was taken to her office.

She had a desk, a desk chair, a bookshelf, a small table with two chairs in the corner . . . and nothing else. No plants. No books. No manuals. No window. No computer. And the phone wasn't connected yet.

Her boss was at a conference that day. He called and left a voicemail (her phone didn't work, remember?), welcoming her to the team and asking if they could meet when he got back into the office in two days.

She said it took a week to get the phone working and to get her laptop.

How did she feel about her orientation? She said, "I felt like they were disorganized. I know they were happy I was on board, but it was a hassle to get everything I needed."

An executive from a different client shared his orientation experiences with me. His first job at the company, 10 years before, was managing a project team. There were a dozen people starting work that day, so they had a daylong orientation. Besides the forms and policy overview they got a campus tour, were shown where to park, got their company IDs and parking passes, and were shown where their cubicles were located.

"A couple of senior executives came in to welcome us and answer questions," he recalled. "It was a nearly perfect orientation day."

Nearly perfect. The flaw in the experience was the closing speaker. The CEO came in for the last 10 minutes of their day. The CEO wasn't comfortable speaking in front of the group (or any group, the executive discovered later). The CEO said, quietly, "I made a video." One of the facilitators started the video, which was of the CEO welcoming new hires.

The CEO read the script to the camera in a halting, stilted manner. He was obviously out of his element, but he did the best he could. At the end of the three-minute clip, the CEO said, "Thank you. I'm sorry."

And walked out of the room.

The executive said, "We were stunned. We didn't know the CEO at all but didn't expect him to be so uncomfortable. He made *us* uncomfortable."

It was an odd closing to an otherwise very successful and helpful orientation day.

Over time, they learned that the CEO was a terrific, visionary leader who was extremely introverted. The CEO loved discussions with one or two people at a time. He just struggled to communicate effectively to larger groups—and to the camera.

The moral of these stories is that the way you treat new hires tells them more about your purpose, values, and culture than anything you say.

Make sure there are a variety of ways new hires can get the guidance and support they need, so they can be successful and fit into the culture effectively.

There are some basic elements of an effective orientation and integration approach. They include culture exposure, mentoring, partnering with the boss, and contribution management.

Culture Exposure

Culture exposure is the intentional and conscious education and guidance of new hires in the ways of your organizational constitution. Like your own leaders and team members before you brought the organizational constitution into your department, your new leaders and team members are unlikely to have had any experience in previous roles and companies with values alignment.

Help ground them in your formal purpose, values and behaviors, strategies, and goals. Help them understand how great team citizens look, act, and sound. Model the valued behaviors with them consistently.

Engage their teams in regular discussion about values alignment. Celebrate great values interactions, and study ways to increase values alignment in day-to-day interactions. (Remember that Ritz-Carlton shares values-alignment stories and examines one of its 12 service values in an all-employee meeting at the start of *every day*.)

Let new hires know about your twice-a-year custom values survey, where leaders and team members are rated on the degree to which they model your valued behaviors daily.

These activities will help embed your organizational constitution into new hires' daily practices. (These practices will also help embed your organizational constitution into current leaders' and team members' daily practices!)

Mentoring

Assign every new leader and team member a mentor. This mentor should be someone other than his or her formal supervisor. Having a mentor outside the reporting relationship can offer a safe avenue for new hires to ask "stupid questions" or to seek guidance on any aspect of their work life.

Mentoring is designed to help provide the new hire with insights on job knowledge, culture reinforcement, strategic clarity, and problem solving.

Mentoring begins with an hour-long meeting every couple of weeks with the focus on what the new hire wants to discuss. After two months of scheduled meetings, the new hire can request a meeting with his or her mentor as needed.

Mentors shall not address personnel or human resources issues— you already have trained team members in place to do that well.

Mentoring programs can help new hires navigate their work life, and you will also find that current leaders and team members would love access to mentoring, as well.

Partnering with the Boss

The primary impression that new hires have of your team or department comes from their relationship with their boss. The secondary impression comes from their fellow team members.

Crafting a formal partnership between the new hire and his or her leader ensures that the new hire:

- Understands both his or her performance expectations and values expectations

- Gains guidance and encouragement from the boss regularly

- Has access to the boss for questions, validation of effort, and so on

The boss needs to embrace his or her responsibility to be a servant leader, to provide the new hires with the help they need to contribute consistently to the team's success.

With a servant-leader mind-set, the boss can help his or her partnership with the new hire evolve smoothly and gratifyingly for both parties.

Contribution Management

As discussed earlier in this book, *contribution management* is my terminology for performance management. Contribution management helps underscore the requirement to plan the new hires' performance expectations as well as their values expectations for the coming year.

Contribution planning outlines clear goals and performance metrics plus the values metrics required by all leaders and team members. The plan then becomes the map for the new hire's partnership with the boss.

As goals are achieved and new goals are formulated, the contribution plan is updated so it's current, every day. When contribution evaluation comes around, it is a simple matter for both parties to review the year (or six-month period) and agree on accomplishments, missed targets, and values alignment.

Contribution management is a series of conversations that happen often. The new hire is never at a loss to understand where he or she stands on performance targets and values demonstration.

There may be other elements you would include in ongoing orientation and integration, but these are the pieces that best practices companies consistently implement.

WHAT IF THE NEW HIRE JUST DOESN'T FIT?

Is it possible that, after all your terrific orientation and integration activities, a new hire just doesn't fit the culture or the performance demands as you expected?

Some new practices are emerging, led by Zappos, a company we've discussed before in this book. At the end of a four-week orientation program, Zappos makes a "pay to quit" offer[5] to every new hire. The company offers new hires $2,000 to quit, before they get started. Why?

The company wants every employee to be at Zappos because they want to be and because they believe in the Zappos culture. If new hires know they don't quite mesh with the culture, the company doesn't want them to feel stuck there.

Less than 2 percent of new hires take Zappos up on the offer.

Zappos's parent company, Amazon, began offering a similar "pay to quit" program[6] in 2013 for fulfillment center employees. Once a year, Amazon offers to pay fulfillment center associates to quit. The first year the offer is made, it's for $2,000. Then it goes up $1,000 a year until it reaches $5,000.

Jeff Bezos, Amazon founder and CEO, said in his letter to shareholders, "We hope they don't take the offer. We want them to stay. The goal is to encourage folks to . . . think about what they really want. An employee staying somewhere they don't want to be isn't healthy for the employee or the company."

It's a bold and brilliant idea. If a new hire who is a culture misfit stays on, it's only a matter of time before the employee's values disconnects cause conflict or uproar. Addressing the uproar is expensive.

It takes time and energy. Replacing the bad hire is expensive—recruiting, interviewing, and orienting costs money. And it will take time before the replacement hire is fully contributing!

If an existing Amazon fulfillment center associate isn't fulfilled (pun intended) by the work at the center, the associate is not going to be as productive or as good a team citizen over time.

Offering new hires the chance to leave Zappos before they engage in a lousy culture fit or to leave Amazon's fulfillment centers because they want to do something else—and pay them $2,000 or even $5,000— is much less expensive than the alternative.

In addition, it protects the high-performing, values-aligned players already in place.

CHAPTER 10

Don't Leave Your Organizational Culture to Chance

I magine a small pond. A log juts out from the water near the shoreline. Five frogs are sitting on the log. Four decide to jump off.

How many frogs are left on the log?

Five. Deciding to jump doesn't mean they've jumped! *Deciding* and *doing* are two very different things.

It's time now for *you* to jump.

It's time to take your good work and implement these practices so you, your leaders, and your team members enjoy a high-performing, values-aligned work environment.

My goal for this book is to educate and inspire leaders to be intentional about purpose, values and behaviors, strategies, and goals . . . to make values alignment as important as goal accomplishment . . . to make workplace inspiration a common occurrence, not a rarity.

We've learned that culture by default doesn't generate consistent performance, customer service, employee inspiration, or profits.

Culture by design, however, *can* generate those desired outcomes.

Implementing an organizational constitution helps boost passion, people, and performance. Our culture clients have consistently experienced 40 percent or greater gains in employee engagement, 40 percent or greater gains in customer satisfaction, and 35 percent or greater profit growth, typically in less than 18 months.

Once employees see that leaders are serious about creating a values-aligned work environment, those employees proactively apply discretionary energy toward company goals, customers, and opportunities.

Discretionary energy means employees *choose* to be present, choose to proactively solve problems, and choose to engage in their team and the company's success.

Here's an example of how generating employee discretionary energy can make a huge positive impact on the business. One client, a $40 million business, experienced compression of revenues during the global recession. The high-performance, values-aligned work environment had reached its limit. If savings couldn't be generated, the next step was to lay off valued, long-term employees.

Employees rallied to the challenge. Within weeks, employees presented cost-cutting suggestions that ultimately led to nearly $1 million in annual savings! No layoffs occurred.

That's outstanding. And my consultant mind looks at this from a different perspective. Why hadn't these suggestions popped up before this crisis? Apparently employees had watched the company overspend on those practices for *years*. Only when the culture requested and enabled it—and the company's survival depended on it—did employees come forward with their terrific suggestions.

When you manage your team or department by an organizational constitution, you put proven practices into place that align skills and values for the benefit of shareholders, employees, and customers.

The Culture Effectiveness Assessment for this chapter gauges how strong workplace inspiration (and alignment to an organizational constitution) is in your team or department.

You've learned that you need to start from a firm foundation about who you are as a person, in whatever role you embrace in life—at home, in your community, at work, wherever.

Consequently, you've crafted a draft of your personal purpose and personal values and behaviors. You've put some time into considering

Culture Effectiveness Assessment #10: Workplace Inspiration	Strongly Disagree	Disagree	Slightly Disagree	Slightly Agree	Agree	Strongly Agree
1. **Team Leaders and Members Are Proud** People on our team or in our department are proud of the team and the work we do. They sport logo wear in the community and speak positively about working here.	1	2	3	4	5	6
2. **Values and Behaviors Are Valued** Leaders and team members are enthused about their values-aligned work environment. They celebrate alignment and refine values missteps daily.	1	2	3	4	5	6
3. **Shared Goals Are Clear** Leaders and team members are of one heart, one mind, and one voice regarding performance targets and customer service excellence.	1	2	3	4	5	6
4. **Servant Leadership Is Apparent** Leaders are seen by leaders and team members as servant leaders, removing hurdles, validating efforts, and serving unselfishly.	1	2	3	4	5	6
5. **Customers Notice Team Members' Enthusiasm** Internal and external customers experience great service from positive, aligned team members and express gratitude for it.	1	2	3	4	5	6

your leadership philosophy, clarifying your servant leadership strategy for leading others effectively and kindly.

You've also learned a great deal about the elements of an organizational constitution—your team or department's purpose, values and behaviors, strategies, and goals. You understand why those elements are important to team performance and to team trust and respect.

You've probably begun developing your organizational constitution, creating drafts of your business purpose, values, valued behaviors, strategic opportunities, and goals that support those strategies.

Your commitment to implement an organizational constitution has been building.

The great news is you're smarter about culture. Your thinking has, it is hoped, evolved toward the "I need to do this with my team" camp.

More great news: you can't go back to being dumb about the impact of your team's culture on team member engagement, customer service, and profits!

LONG-TERM ALIGNMENT VERSUS SHORT-TERM RESULTS

As you embark on the implementation of your organizational constitution, realize that you'll be presenting a different way of thinking about the work the team does. You'll be asking people to shift away from a "short-term, results *now*" mind-set to a "long-term, inspiring workplace that delivers great products and services" mind-set.

You'll need to invest time and energy in educating leaders and team members why this long-term approach is a great thing for your team or department. You'll need to bring people along, day by day, praising aligned plans, decisions, and actions and redirecting misaligned ones.

The time and energy that you continue to invest ensure that this initiative doesn't suffer from the plague of MbA—managing by announcements.

You will need to help leaders and team members understand that your organizational constitution doesn't *reduce* the emphasis on performance standards; it *clarifies* them with aligned strategies and goals. You'll help them understand that the organizational constitution adds a new dimension to what a good job looks like: great team citizenship and values alignment.

SCORING YOUR CULTURE EFFECTIVENESS ASSESSMENT

Let's take a few minutes to score your Culture Effectiveness Assessment (CEA). Each of the 10 chapters in the book—including this chapter—presents five best practices for you to rate using your current team or department.

The rating scale is a 1- to 6-point range, using a continuum from "strongly disagree" (scored a 1) to "strongly agree" (scored a 6). What are desirable scores? You want everyone in the department to rate these best practices at the 5 or 6 level— "agree" or "strongly agree."

There are 50 items (or questions) on the CEA. The maximum score per item is 6, which means the total possible points is 300 (a "perfect game" for bowling fans).

Your point total reflects the quality and condition of your current team or department's organizational culture. There are five quality levels, which I shared with you in Chapter 1. They include:

- **Dysfunction.** This is the lowest quality level, indicating a culture of low trust, inconsistent performance, and consistent frustration when trying to get things done.

- **Tension.** This is the second-lowest quality level. Trust is still not present. Performance is slightly better but remains inconsistent. Disagreements occur regularly, but overt conflict is not as common.

- **Civility.** This is the middle ground, and represents the minimum desired standard of culture quality. All leaders and team members are treated with respect. Interactions are formal and professional. Performance is consistently good. Disagreements about ideas are conducted calmly without denigrating the leader or team member's commitment, skills, and role.

- **Acknowledgment.** This quality level is reflected in the active recognition and expression of thanks and gratitude for effort, accomplishment, service, and citizenship. Performance is very good. Customers are treated respectfully. The phrase "thank you" is heard a lot.

- **Validation.** This quality level demands the active valuing of team members' ideas, skills, enthusiasm, and talent. Leaders delegate authority and responsibility to talented and engaged team members.

Your CEA point total is a strong indication of the quality level of your team or department culture.

A score of **99 points** or less indicates your team or department culture is at the **dysfunction** quality level.

A score of **100 to 149 points** indicates the **tension** quality level for your culture.

Scores that range between **150 and 199 points** reflect the **civility** quality level for your culture.

A score of **200 to 249 points** indicates that your team or department culture is at the **acknowledgment** quality level.

A score of **250 to 300 points** indicates the **validation** quality level for your culture.

What we know is that teams and departments that implement and align to an organizational constitution enjoy a validating culture. That quality level is reflected in team member engagement, customers being wowed consistently, and growing profits over time.

Your score tally will give you a very good indication of your team or department culture quality today. You can invite others in your department to complete the CEA, as well, to gain additional perspectives.

To some extent, though, focusing primarily on your CEA scores is like weighing yourself each day. The numbers tell a part of the story. If you want to add muscle to your body, you need to do the work to add muscle. Your scale will tell you if you're gaining weight, but it won't tell you if you're gaining muscle. You'd need to do other testing (endurance, speed, strength, etc.) to gain reliable data on muscle growth.

So, tally your CEA scores and understand what quality level your team or department culture is at. Then, set the CEA aside, and engage in the work of implementing your organizational constitution. That will result in the greatest gains in values alignment, inspiration, teamwork, and performance.

IMPLEMENTING AN ORGANIZATIONAL CONSTITUTION IS AN ONGOING PROJECT

Creating, socializing, publishing, and aligning people and practices to your organizational constitution is a long-term proposition. It's a project that basically never goes away.

You'll make terrific strides in the first 18 to 24 months. Plans, decisions, and actions will align to your organizational constitution. You'll see growth in profits, engagement, and service.

And there will always be opportunities to do better. You'll bring in new players who will need coaching and redirecting. You might enter new markets and face a different client base or needed skill set or business pace.

The old ways of doing business—the norm for many businesses today—will always be a temptation. You must be ever vigilant to keep your team or department on its unique path as defined by your organizational constitution.

Project planning for your organizational constitution needs to be as thorough and detailed as for any other major project that your team or department undertakes.

You probably have existing systems in your department to track project commitments and activities. If not, there are some terrific software tools now available, some of which I use daily. For example, right now I use Nozbe[1] (to manage daily tasks); Evernote[2] (to manage project notes, images, and voice recordings); and Asana[3] (a terrific web-based project management application with tablet and smartphone apps). I'm constantly testing new tools; view my updated list on my website at drtc.me/tools.

From this book, you already know the important elements required to implement the organizational constitution process. They include, in chronological order:

1. Clarifying your personal purpose, values and behaviors, and refining and sharing your leadership philosophy (from Chapter 2)

2. Writing a draft of your organization's business purpose, values, and behaviors (Chapters 3 and 4)

3. Crafting a suggested set of business strategies with specific, aligned goals for the year (Chapter 5)

4. Engaging other leaders in your department in the need for an organizational constitution (Chapters 3, 4, and 5)

5. Engaging other department leaders in the refinement of and additions to your draft organizational constitution (Chapters 3, 4, and 5)

6. Describing the way—communicating and marketing the elements of your organizational constitution, inviting feedback, and publishing and reinforcing it (Chapter 6)

7. Modeling the way—leaders creating credibility for the new values and behaviors by demonstrating them daily, in every interaction (Chapter 6)

8. Aligning the way—leaders celebrating aligned behaviors from other leaders and from team members, and redirecting misaligned behaviors to build consistent demonstration of your organizational constitution (Chapters 6 and 8)

9. Creating a custom values survey to measure behavioral alignment by leaders (Chapter 7)

10. Aligning hiring and orientation practices to ensure values alignment of anyone brought into the team or department (Chapter 9)

Note that work on items 6 to 10 never ends. These alignment efforts are ongoing, ad nauseam!

There is one additional task I would suggest: Identify key metrics you *want* changed and that you believe aligning to your organizational constitution *will* change. The obvious and highly desirable metrics include profitability, customer service, and employee engagement.

Clients have identified additional desirable metrics that they believe aligning to their organizational constitution will positively impact. Those have included new product development, market share of products less than three years old, team self-directedness, and being a great company to work for (metrics might include those on Glassdoor.com or inclusion in a regional "great company" recognition list each year).

You can implement these 10 project elements in a small, intact team entirely on your own. You don't need anyone's permission to craft a team organizational constitution and align players and practices to it.

If your sphere of influence is larger than a small, intact team, you would leverage these same 10 practices in the same order. The larger scope simply means you'll have more leaders to engage, more education to conduct, and a larger number of players to align—but the core pieces are the same.

My wish for you is that you engage in this process—that you implement an organizational constitution in your sphere of influence.

This world needs teams and companies that have safe, inspiring work environments that team members love. This proven path awaits you.

Keep Me Informed

I welcome your questions and comments about this process. I am active on Twitter (@scedmonds), Facebook (DrivingResultsThrough-Culture), LinkedIn (chrisedmonds), and Google + (+SChrisEdmonds) and at drivingresultsthroughculture.com.

To subscribe to my weekly posts and podcasts, and get access to free resources and insights, go to drtc.me/sub1.

To check out updates and resources for this book, go to thecultureengine.com.

For information about executive consulting and culture change process coaching, contact me at drivingresultsthroughculture.com.

Enjoy this gratifying journey!

Notes

Introduction

1. Stephen R. Covey, Business Mission Statements, www.stephencovey.com/mission-statements.php.
2. Marcus Luttrell, *Lone Survivor* (New York: Little, Brown, 2007).

Chapter 1: What Is an Organizational Constitution, and Why Do You Need One?

1. OnRec, "Monster Global Poll Reveals Workplace Bullying Is Endemic," On Recruitment, June 2011, www.onrec.com/news/news-archive/monster-global-poll-reveals-workplace-bullying-is-endemic.
2. Canadian Centre for Occupational Health and Safety, "Bullying in the Workplace," www.ccohs.ca/oshanswers/psychosocial/bullying.html.
3. Margaret J. Wheatley and Geoff Crinean, "Solving, Not Attacking, Complex Problems," 2004, www.margaretwheatley.com/articles/solving notattacking.html.
4. The "Performance-Values Matrix" was originally published in the *"Gung Ho!" Participant Workbook*, Item #10832, © 2000 Blanchard Family Partnership and Ode to Joy Limited, and is included herein with the authors' permission.
5. S. Chris Edmonds, "Performance-Values Assessment," drivingresults throughculture.com/research.
6. S. Chris Edmonds, "Great Boss Assessment," drivingresultsthroughcul ture.com/research.
7. Zappos, culture book, zapposinsights.com/culture-book.
8. WorldBlu, Democratic Workplace awards, worldblu.com/democratic-design.
9. Gallup, Inc., "2013 State of the American Workplace," www.gallup.com/strategicconsulting/163007/state-american-workplace.aspx.
10. Gallup, Inc., Q-12 Meta-Analysis, strengths.gallup.com/private/Resources/Q12Meta-Analysis_Flyer_GEN_08%2008_BP.pdf.
11. Kenexa Research Institute, "The Impact of Employee Engagement," white paper, www.kenexa.com/getattachment/8c36e336-3935-4406-8b7b-777f1afaa57d/The-Impact-of-Employee-Engagement.aspx.

12. Gallup, Inc., "2010 State of the Global Workplace," www.gallup.com /strategicconsulting/157196/state-global-workplace.aspx.

13. Tony Simons, *The Integrity Dividend* (San Francisco: Jossey-Bass, 2008), integritydividend.com.

14. Lynn Cowart, Beverly Crowell, and Beverly Kaye, "Engagement Leaders to Growth at Morrison," *Talent Management*, talentmgt.com/articles /view/engagement-leads-to-growth-at-morrison.

15. Jennifer Robison, "A Caterpillar Dealer Unearths Employee Engagement," *Gallup Business Journal*, October 2006, businessjournal.gallup.com/content /24874/a-caterpillar-dealer-unearths-employee-engagement.aspx#1.

16. Corporate Leadership Council, "Driving Performance and Retention through Employee Engagement," 2004, www.mckpeople.com.au/Site Media/w3svc161/Uploads/Documents/760af459-93b3-43c7-b52a-2a74e984c1a0.pdf.

17. SHRM Foundation, "Employee Engagement and Commitment," 2006, www.shrm.org/about/foundation/news/documents/1006employeeenga gementonlinereport.doc.

18. S. Chris Edmonds with Lisa Zigarmi, Positivity Works, featuring *#Positivity at Work Tweet*, positivity-works.com.

19. Shawn Achor, "Positive Intelligence," *Harvard Business Review*, January/ February 2012.

20. Tom Rath and Jim Harter, "The Economics of Wellbeing," Gallup, Inc., 2010, www.ofyp.umn.edu/ofypmedia/focusfy/The_Economics_of_ Wellbeing.pdf.

21. Ibid. 13.

22. Ibid. 13.

23. Ibid. 14.

24. Ibid. 6.

Chapter 2: It Starts with YOU

1. Mark Deterding, Triune Leadership Services, www.triuneleadershipser vices.com/.

2. National Institutes of Health, body mass index calculator, www.nhlbi.nih .gov/guidelines/obesity/BMI/bmicalc.htm.

3. Timothy Ferriss, "The Four-Hour Body Slow Carb Diet," Gizmodo, gizmodo.com/5709913/4-hour-body—the-slow-carb-diet/all.

4. David Perlmutter, *Grain Brain* (New York: Little, Brown, 2013), www .drperlmutter.com/about/grain-brain-by-david-perlmutter/.

5. NPD Group, *Morning Mealscape* study, www.npd.com/wps/portal/npd/us /news/press-releases/pr_111011b/.

6. Lisa Collier Cool, "The Surprising Dangers of Skipping Breakfast," Yahoo! Healthline, July 23, 2013, health.yahoo.net/experts/dayinhealth /surprising-dangers-skipping-breakfast.

7. Timothy Ferriss, "Make a Healthy Breakfast in Under 3 Minutes," www .youtube.com/watch?v=fd-7a_wdVZk.

8. Kelly Botham, "The Power of Walking: Little Steps, Big Reward," *USA Today*, September 20, 2012, www.usaweekend.com/article/20120921 /HEALTH03/309210006/.

9. *Consumer Reports*, "Activity Trackers," www.consumerreports.org/cro /activity-trackers.htm.

CHAPTER 3: CLARIFY YOUR ORGANIZATION'S PURPOSE

1. Nature Publishing Group, www.nature.com/npg_/company_info/mission .html.

2. Mark Smith et al., "Do Missions Accomplish Their Missions?" from the *Journal of Applied Management and Entrepreneurship*, 2001, www .huizenga.nova.edu/Jame/articles/mission-statement-content.cfm.

3. Cooper Tire & Rubber Company, coopertire.com/About-Us/Our -Company.aspx.

4. Darden Restaurants, www.darden.com/about/faq.asp.

5. Bristol-Myers Squibb, www.bms.com/ourcompany/mission/Pages/default .aspx.

6. Starbucks, www.starbucks.com/about-us/company-information/mission -statement.

7. Newmont Mining Corporation, www.newmont.com/about/company -glance.

8. Institute for Corporate Productivity, "Secret Mission?," www.i4cp.com /news/2008/09/10/secret-mission.

9. Dick Carozza, "Interview with Sherron Watkins," *Fraud Magazine*, January/February 2007, www.fraud-magazine.com/article.aspx?id=583.

10. Accounting Degree Review, "The 10 Worst Corporate Accounting Scandals of All Time," AccountingDegree.org, www.accounting-degree .org/scandals/.

11. Daniel H. Pink, *Drive* (New York: Riverhead Publishing, Penguin Group, 2011).

12. Oprah Winfrey, Super Soul Sunday, "Building a Business with Soul," Oprah Winfrey and Starbucks CEO Howard Schultz, www.oprah.com/ own-super-soul-sunday/Oprah-and-Starbucks-CEO-Howard-Schultz- Building-a-Business-With-Soul.

13. Chris Edmonds Music, chris-edmonds-music.com.

CHAPTER 4: DEFINE VALUES IN BEHAVIORAL TERMS

1. Southwest Cares, www.southwest.com/assets/pdfs/corporate-commitments/southwestcares.pdf; Zappos Core Values, about.zappos.com/jobs/why-work-zappos/core-values.
2. S. Chris Edmonds, The Performance-Values Assessment, drivingresults throughculture.com/research.
3. Jim Taylor, "Technology: Myth of Multitasking," *Psychology Today*, March 30, 2011, www.psychologytoday.com/blog/the-power-prime/201103/technology-myth-multitasking.
4. Goldman Sachs, Business Principles, www.goldmansachs.com/who-we-are/business-standards/business-principles/index.html.
5. Securities and Exchange Commission, "Goldman Sachs to Pay Record $550 Million to Settle Charges Related to Subprime Mortgage CDO," July 15, 2010, www.sec.gov/news/press/2010/2010-123.htm.

CHAPTER 5: OUTLINE STRATEGIES AND GOALS FOR THE COMING FISCAL YEAR

1. University of Scranton, *Journal of Clinical Psychology*, January 2014, reported on Statistic Brain, www.statisticbrain.com/new-years-resolution-statistics/.
2. "Best Goal Setting Apps," AppAdvice, appadvice.com/appguides/show/habit-building-apps.
3. Jim Collins, author, speaker, and researcher, www.jimcollins.com/.

CHAPTER 6: YOUR ORGANIZATIONAL CONSTITUTION MUST BE LIVED

1. For the purposes of this example, we'll suppose you are indeed a department head. The same approach would be used for a division leader, plant manager, company CEO, and so on.
2. Asda (one of the United Kingdom's top retailers), "Experience Asda," www.asda.jobs/experienceAsda.
3. Ritz-Carlton, Gold Standards, corporate.ritzcarlton.com/en/About/Gold Standards.htm.
4. Josh Bersin, "Time to Scrap Performance Appraisals?" *Forbes*, May 6, 2013, www.forbes.com/sites/joshbersin/2013/05/06/time-to-scrap-performance-appraisals/.

5. Ken Blanchard and Garry Ridge, *Helping People Win at Work* (Upper Saddle River, NJ: FT Press, 2009), www.kenblanchard.com/helppeople winatwork/

CHAPTER 7: GATHERING FORMAL FEEDBACK ON VALUED BEHAVIORS

1. FluidSurveys online survey administration, fluidsurveys.com.
2. Cvent online registration and survey administration, www.cvent.com.

CHAPTER 8: DEALING WITH RESISTANCE

1. Marcus Luttrell, *Lone Survivor* (New York: Little, Brown, 2007), marcus luttrell.com/store/lone-survivor-hard-back-autographed-copy/

CHAPTER 9: HIRING FOR VALUES ALIGNMENT

1. Anya Kamenetz, "Warby Parker Co-CEO Neil Blumenthal on Doubling Down on Culture," *Fast Company*, www.fastcompany.com/3003076/warby -parker-co-ceo-neil-blumenthal-doubling-down-culture.
2. Ryan Holmes, "The Unexpectedly High Cost of a Bad Hire," www .linkedin.com/today/post/article/20130716151946-2967511-the-high- costs-of-a-bad-hire-and-how-to-avoid-them.
3. Warby Parker, online glasses retailer, www.warbyparker.com/do-good/ #home.
4. The Mission Continues, community service opportunities for returning military veterans, www.missioncontinues.org/about/.
5. Zappos.com, "Is It True That Zappos Offers New Hires $2,000 to Quit?," about.zappos.com/it-true-zappos-offers-new-hires-2000-quit.
6. G. Chambers Williams III, "Why Is Amazon Paying Workers Up to $5K to Quit?" *USA Today*, www.usatoday.com/story/money/business/2014/04 /10/amazon-pay-to-quit/7560259/.

CHAPTER 10: DON'T LEAVE YOUR ORGANIZATIONAL CULTURE TO CHANCE

1. Nozbe, task management application, nozbe.com.
2. Evernote, note-taking archival and retrieval applications, evernote .com.
3. Asana, project management application, asana.com.

ABOUT THE AUTHOR

S. Chris Edmonds is the founder and CEO of The Purposeful Culture Group.

After a 15-year career leading and managing successful business teams, Chris began his consulting company in 1990. Since 1995, he has also served as a senior consultant with the Ken Blanchard Companies.

Chris has delivered leadership training to thousands of clients, facilitated strategic planning and chartering sessions for hundreds of executive teams, provided executive consulting and coaching to hundreds of executives, and presented nearly 200 keynotes to rave reviews from audiences of 100–5,000.

Over the years, Chris has worked for clients in industries including automotive, banking and financial services, government, hospitality, insurance, manufacturing, non-profit, pharmaceutical, retail, sales, software, and technology.

Under Chris' guidance, culture clients have consistently boosted their customer satisfaction by 40 percent or more, employee engagement by 40 percent or more, and their profits by 30 percent or more.

Chris is the author or co-author of six books, including Ken Blanchard's best-selling revised and enhanced edition of *Leading at a Higher Level*. His ChangeThis manifesto, titled, "What? Your Organization Doesn't Have a Constitution?" is available free at drtc.me/chng.

He received his master's degree from the University of San Francisco in human resource and organizational development and is an adjunct professor at the University of San Diego School of Business.

Chris has thousands of Twitter, Facebook, LinkedIn, and Google+ followers who look forward to his leadership, culture, and values quotes every day.

His blogs, podcasts, leadership and culture assessments, and analysis of his research findings are available at www.DrivingResults ThroughCulture.com.

Subscribe to his blog and podcast updates at www.drtc.me/sub1 and get access to free resources and updates each week.

Chris is an accomplished musician and performer. He provides guitar, banjo, mandolin, and vocals for Graystone Records recording artist, the Jones & Raine band. Two singles from the band's 2009 debut album made the Billboard country charts. Learn more about Chris' musician life at chris-edmonds-music.com.

Chris lives with his wife, Diane, and their flatcoat retriever, Shady, at 8,400 feet above sea level in Conifer, Colorado.

Index